THE CUP OF COFFEE CLUB

THE CUP OF COFFEE CLUB

11 Players and Their Brush with Baseball History

Jacob Kornhauser

ROWMAN & LITTLEFIELD
Lanham • Boulder • New York • London

Published by Rowman & Littlefield
An imprint of The Rowman & Littlefield Publishing Group, Inc.
4501 Forbes Boulevard, Suite 200, Lanham, Maryland 20706
www.rowman.com

86-90 Paul Street, London EC2A 4NE, United Kingdom

British Library Cataloguing in Publication Information Available

Library of Congress Cataloging-in-Publication Data

Names: Kornhauser, Jacob, 1994– author.
Title: The cup of coffee club : 11 players and their brush with baseball history / Jacob
    Kornhauser.
Description: Lanham, Maryland : Rowman & Littlefield, 2020. | Includes bibliographical
    references and index. | Summary: "Most baseball players will never reach the major
    leagues. While many that do stay there for a long time, there are a select few that
    played in just one major league game. Cup of Coffee Club tells the stories of eleven of
    these players and their struggles to reach the major leagues, as well as their struggles
    to get back"—Provided by publisher.
Identifiers: LCCN 2019038836 (print) | LCCN 2019038837 (ebook) | ISBN
    9781538130810 (cloth) | ISBN 9781538175453 (paperback) | ISBN 9781538130827
    (ebook)
Subjects: LCSH: Baseball players—United States—Biography. | Minor league
    baseball—United States. | Major League Baseball (Organization)
Classification: LCC GV865.A1 K68 2020 (print) | LCC GV865.A1 (ebook) | DDC
    796.357092/ 273—dc23
LC record available at https://lccn.loc.gov/2019038836
LC ebook record available at https://lccn.loc.gov/2019038837

CONTENTS

FOREWORD

This is a collection of singular performances, yet to understand these performances by the singular event would be a narrow understanding. How each fared at the plate, how many Ks each recorded, who got a hit or who notched a goose egg—that's not the point here. In the "Cup of Coffee Club," the game itself is the head of a pin; if you look at it head-on, you're not seeing most of the thing, just one point on it. Therein lies the life of these stories: though these men are tied together in a peculiar class of ballplayers, they are also tied together in a much more meaningful way.

The accounts in this book may seem to start and end in very different ways at first glance. Some are groomed for the game while others fall in love with it organically. Some remain with baseball for decades after their one game, while others find success in realms far from a baseball diamond. In every case, however, one thing is the same: the dream.

To some, the relationship of some of these men to the game they love may seem one sided. In youth, they give it a lifetime of toil, and of sacrifice. They allow it to define them. They become competitors. And in the days after baseball, they give it endless moments of reflection and, in some cases, regret. In return, they each get one single game. This transaction could appear lopsided, but not to someone who has the dream.

This book contains statistics; but in baseball—as in life—the stats don't tell the whole story. Thus, this is not a two-dollar program, peddled by a barker outside Wrigley Field on a Sunday afternoon in June. It is not a book of 11 box scores; etched on these pages is the story of 11 dreamers, and the entire lives that form around a baseball dream.

The most intriguing aspect of this collection is its protagonists themselves. Some have names you've heard. Some have watched relatives and siblings emblazon their names in baseball legend. Others have gone on to greatness in other areas of the game. None of the players chose to play just a single game, and each valiantly clung to the dream of succeeding in the game, but ultimately these are stories of reality. That being said, these are all still stories of success. The circumstances around the protagonists' exit from baseball do not involve a lot of choice, but the stories told here show how every complete narrative reveals itself as a series of choices. The men who inspired this work decided to be ballplayers, and each subsequent decision that would define their lives comes as a consequence of that one vital choice. This is a group of men who, for better or worse, lived the dream. This is the Cup of Coffee Club.

—Dylan Kornhauser, editor

ACKNOWLEDGMENTS

As an MLB career does, making a book like this work requires the faith and hard work of a lot of individual work outside of the writer's vision and execution. First of all, a huge thank-you to every single player who made themselves available to me and opened up about their big-league career. For many, this was not an easy topic and they trusted me to tell their stories. For that, I will always be appreciative. Thank you also to the many other experts I talked to, who provided amazing background information to help the story come to life.

The person who provided me the most guidance throughout this entire process was Ken Samelson. He was a fantastic mentor as I went through the publishing process, and he went out of his way to help me even though he had nothing to personally gain from my success. I will forever be indebted to Ken for helping me get my first book published. Rick Wolff, similarly, did not have any personal reason to help me but did. He has more experience in the publishing world than anyone I've met, and he was willing to impart that wisdom to me, because he believed in a young author and the vision for a baseball book.

My family and loved ones were vital to the success of this book as well. Dylan, my younger brother and editor, helped this story come to life. He's made my words sound better and the themes pop, and the book as a whole has improved tremendously under his watchful eye. It has always been a dream of ours to work on a writing project together and this is just the first of many. Both of my parents, Ari and Angela, have always been supportive of my writing, and without that support early on,

I would not have had the confidence to take on a writing project of this magnitude.

Of course, I must thank my beautiful girlfriend, Khaki, who has been by my side since the idea for this book popped into my head at her apartment one fateful day in 2017. Her love and support mean the world to me and helped give me the strength to keep writing even when months passed without any interviews being set up. My friend Corey Miller also deserves a lot of credit for having to listen to me bounce random ideas off him. He might be a die-hard baseball fan, but I bombarded him with so many ideas, I'm sure he got tired of it at some point. Nevertheless, he has been there from start to finish to provide his insight on the project, and I am very thankful for that.

A few of my mentors deserve mention here as well. John Anderson, a fellow University of Missouri alum, has taken me under his wing over the past couple years and I couldn't be more appreciative. Having someone as successful as him at ESPN pay attention to and care about what I'm doing professionally has given me the confidence to continue taking on projects like this in the future. I have a deep gratitude for the tutelage of Tim Kurkjian as well. He was one of my childhood writing idols; I read just about every word he wrote about baseball growing up. To be able to meet him and have him now periodically critique my work is a dream come true.

It is also worth noting that Baseball Reference has been unbelievably helpful in this project. Without that resource, this book might not exist. Frankly, I'm not sure how baseball books were researched before the dawn of Baseball Reference. Then again, I'm a millennial, and probably would have just had to struggle in that thing they call a library. The Society for American Baseball Research was also an incredibly helpful tool, especially in providing biographical information on some of the older, more obscure players mentioned in the book. Their attention to detail made my job of storytelling a lot easier.

Finally, I owe a huge thank-you to Christen Karniski and the team at Rowman & Littlefield. Like aspiring big-league players need a general manager and support system that believe in them to make it to the majors, I needed a publisher to believe in the vision of a 24-year-old first-time author. They have done that and given me all the support I need to be successful. Thank you, Christen, for helping me bring my vision to life and trusting baseball fans and others would connect with the stories I told within this book.

INTRODUCTION

The Invisible Battle

What would you give to play one game in the major leagues? To feel the wind at your back, to see the flags blowing at Wrigley Field, to walk past the Green Monster at Fenway Park or glance over at Monument Park at Yankee Stadium? Would you dedicate your entire life to the game, knowing you may never get your moment in the sun, your chance to step onto the field as a big leaguer?

Ask any school-aged boy what he wants to be when he grows up. At some time or another, he will tell you he wants to be a ballplayer. It's a popular dream, just as it was when his father was young and his grandfather before him. How many of those boys, those dads, those granddads, actually got to live that dream? In the organized history of baseball, fewer than 19,000—the equivalent of a medium-sized university's student body.[1]

Against those odds, why does the dream live on? What makes a boy, as he slowly becomes a man, think he can hack it in the big leagues? Well, to be a professional baseball player, you have to be a little crazy. You have to believe in yourself and your ability more than in any other sport. Other sports don't have the rigorous minor leagues to both physically and mentally separate the men from the boys. A baseball player with major-league aspirations doesn't just have to battle an opponent, or even a teammate gunning for his roster spot. He has to battle himself.

Through high school, college, and the minors, very few ever get to live out the childhood dream of playing in the major leagues. For those who do, sometimes the dream is fleeting, one that quickly passes. For others, it's as if they've woken up and wonder if the dream ever happened at all. These are the players who put in tens of thousands of hours of work for a few hours in the major leagues. These are the players who poured their lives into the sport and whose sport became their lives. For these players, their chance on baseball's highest level came and went with almost no notice. This is the small group of big leaguers who played in just one MLB game.

Over the past 50 years, fewer than 150 men have had the distinction as "cup of coffee" players, those who played in just one major-league game.[2] Some had solid outings on the mound and were never given another chance. Others had great days at the plate but never appeared there again.

Others needed the help of veteran teammates to convince a manager to give them a major-league at bat before they were sent back down to the minors. Still more showed a small sample of what they could do but weren't given an extended chance to show if they could stick in the bigs. These players are the modern-day versions of Moonlight Graham.

Moonlight Graham's story was popularized in the hit movie *Field of Dreams*, where the fictional version of Graham opines to Ray Kinsella about his fleeting experience in the major leagues. A doctor in the film, Graham talks to Ray about life and his experience in baseball. Many don't realize Moonlight Graham was a real player (and doctor) and, like the players whose stories will be told firsthand in this book, he played in just one big-league game.

Archie Graham was born on November 12, 1877, in Fayetteville, North Carolina, and went on to attend the University of Maryland, Baltimore, and the University of North Carolina, Chapel Hill. Never leaving the East Coast, Graham was a talented baseball player who ended up being called up by the New York Giants. On June 29, 1905, he made his major-league debut. With the Giants up 11–1 on the Brooklyn Superbas, he was sent out to right field in the eighth inning.

The 27-year-old came back to the dugout after three outs were recorded in the eighth. It was the Giants' turn to bat in the ninth, and Graham would finally get a chance to step into a big-league batter's box. Graham was due up fourth in the inning, though, and when the Giants hitters went three-up, three-down, their right fielder was standing on deck.[3] He was a few paces from living out his dream of getting an at bat in the major leagues, but it appeared that dream would have to wait. The dream, as it happened, never came true.

He was sent back out to right field for the bottom of the ninth inning as the Giants got the final three outs of the game and secured the blowout win. A few days after his debut, Graham was sent back down to the minor leagues, never to return to the majors for his one chance to dig into the dirt of a big-league batter's box.

Famously, in *Field of Dreams*, Graham's character tells Ray:

> You know we just don't recognize the most significant moments of our lives while they're happening. Back then I thought, well, there'll be other days. I didn't realize that that was the only day.[4]

Nobody who gets their first day in the major leagues knows it's their last day in the major leagues too. For most "fringe" baseball players—players who are good enough to play in the big leagues, but not good enough to be an obvious everyday player—reaching the majors is a matter of timing and mental toughness.

While Moonlight Graham may be baseball's most famous cup of coffee player, he was not the first. That distinction goes to a man named Frank Norton, who appeared in the second game in the history of Organized Baseball. He also appears on what is believed to be the country's first known baseball card, posing alongside his 1865 Brooklyn Atlantics teammates.[5] He played for the Washington Olympics of the American Association on May 5, 1871.[6] Right from the dawn of our great pastime, there have been players whose major-league careers turned to dusk just after the sun rose on their professional playing days.

Playing against the Boston Red Stockings in his one career game, Norton stepped up to the plate just once. He struck out. The pitcher that day: Al Spalding, future Hall of Famer and fundamental part of baseball's early days as an executive. He helped organize a baseball world tour in 1889 that saw professional ballplayers playing in the shadows of the Pyramids in Egypt and in front of the king of Italy.[7]

Norton played just two innings that afternoon. In the field, he had one ball hit to him. He made an error. He earned the unfortunate label of being a career .000 hitter and .000 fielder. In a day when pitchers still had to throw the ball underhand, the Red Stockings beat the Olympics 20–18 that May afternoon for the first win in franchise history. Roughly 5,000 people saw Norton's first and only appearance.[8]

Not much is known of Norton, who became the game's first one-day participant, other than the fact he was born June 9, 1845, in Port Jefferson, New York, and died August 1, 1920, in Greenwich, Connecticut, at the age of 75.

Baseball was completely different in Norton's day. It was just scratching the surface of what it would become. The challenges he faced in reaching the majors aren't what young men face today. In general, though, there is one fundamental truth: the most talented bunch of professional players will make it to the major leagues, barring injury, and the least talented bunch won't make it out of A-ball.

Sometimes, it is not the baseball gods who call your number when it's up. Sometimes, that's left to life itself. Dick Wantz, a 25-year-old pitcher for the California Angels, made his major-league debut on April 13, 1965, an Opening Day relief appearance against the Cleveland Indians at Dodger Stadium.[9] This was the last Opening Day on which the Angels and Dodgers would share a home field.[10]

In the top of the eighth, with the Angels trailing 5–0, Wantz was summoned from the bullpen. The first batter he faced was Max Alvis. He struck him out. Then the floodgates opened. Double, double, single, and two more runs had scored, putting the Indians up 7–0. Wantz then struck out Ralph Terry and got Dick Howser to fly out to end the inning. One inning, an 18.00 ERA and Wantz's career was over.[11] It wasn't because his team didn't trust his arm. It was because of what was going on beneath the surface.

A few days after his debut, Wantz was complaining of terrible headaches. A trip to the doctor yielded the worst possible news: Wantz had an inoperable brain tumor. On May 13, exactly one month after he debuted in the big leagues, Wantz underwent surgery in which surgeons tried to remove as much of the bilateral tumor (both sides of the brain) as they could. He never woke up. At just 25 years old, with his entire career in front of him, Wantz was gone.[12]

What happens to the players lucky enough to get the chance to live out their big-league dream? Most who make it out of A-ball are still middle-of-the-pack players who are at the mercy of their own minds, the timing of their careers, and the judgment of key decision makers. It is only players who fall into this category who become one-game wonders.

They might be "fringe" players who overachieved, making their one day in the big leagues a remarkable feat. They could also be players who looked headed for a promising career but had that career derailed, making their status as a footnote in baseball history a major disappointment.

Larry Hines, a former MLB executive, once told a fringe minor-league pitcher, "There are five Randy Johnsons and five David Cones in the world. Then, there are 200 guys just like you. Of those 200, 100 are in the major leagues and 100 are in the minor leagues."[13]

Timing and mental toughness help determine which 100 fall into each category. Many sports psychologists say mental toughness is the biggest separator between someone who will reach the major leagues and someone who won't.

After all, the majority of players, even as high as Triple-A, will never be able to sustain a major-league career. If they were able to admit this to themselves, the minor leagues would run low on players. Former Red Sox manager and longtime minor-league manager Joe Morgan (no relation to the Hall of Fame second baseman) hated having to be the one to give it to his players straight: you aren't going to make it in the major leagues. If he did that with most of the minor leaguers he coached, he wouldn't be able to field a team.[14]

Mike Stadler, cognitive psychologist and author of *The Psychology of Baseball*, points to a case study between Billy Beane and Darryl Strawberry as a prime example of mental toughness separating two similarly talented players.

"Strawberry was just really good at saying, 'Okay, I went 0-for-3, so what?' He would just go back out and do the same thing the next day," Stadler says. "You often hear Billy Beane talk about how he would start to feel claustrophobic in the batter's box. . . . I think there are definitely psychological variables where you have two people with equal ability and one might succeed spectacularly and the other might fail spectacularly. The mental side can be the difference."[15]

There is also something to be said about having a love for the game. If you don't love the game and you aren't a superstar, the game will wear you down. How do you continue to love the game over and over again when it never seems to love you back? If you could turn back time, you might ask relief pitcher Dan Osinski.

After starting his minor-league career in 1952, Osinski put his nose to the grindstone and worked toward his major-league dream. After ten years, he had yet to reach the big leagues. Most players would have moved on by 1962. The life of a minor-league baseball player was tumultuous in those days, even more so than it is today.

Osinski chose to keep fighting toward his dream. He was a carpenter during the offseason and knew he could do that for decades. Baseball was something he could only do in his youth, so he held on for dear life. Eventually, baseball loved Osinski back. He made his major-league debut for the Kansas City Athletics on April 11, 1962.[16]

Osinski got more than one game in the major leagues, though. Making his debut at age 28, he went on to pitch in parts of eight big-league seasons. In 1967, he appeared in relief for the Boston Red Sox in Game Seven of the World Series against the St. Louis Cardinals.[17] His love for the game and unwillingness to quit enabled him to reach baseball's biggest stage 15 years after his professional career began.

The mentality a minor leaguer has to have to keep the major-league dream alive is something that will be touched on in greater detail later, but one thing psychology can't explain is how timing impacts a player's eventual career arc. Did Osinski have good timing, or bad? It took him a decade to reach his dream, but he eventually reached it. The answer to the "good or bad timing" question depends on who you ask; as hard as it may be to accept, though, fringe minor leaguers don't have a great deal of control over whether they eventually reach the big leagues.

When it comes to reaching the bigs, there is a strong external locus of control. That is to say, factors outside of fringe minor leaguers' influence are often of greatest influence to their careers.

To show just how much timing matters for a player's eventual career, consider the case of "Player A"[18] and "Player B"[19] (see tables I.1 and I.2).

So, what kind of career do you think each player had? Clearly, just based on their minor-league numbers, neither was destined to be an MLB star. However, each had a breakout 2005 season, which showed they might have some major-league potential. Overall, though, the early minor-league careers of these two players—which overlapped almost perfectly—were relatively comparable.

"Player A" is Ronny Cedeño. He appeared in 875 MLB games and appeared at the plate 2,792 times across parts of ten seasons with seven different MLB teams.

"Player B" is Chase Lambin. He never appeared in an MLB game.

Table I.1. Player A: Shortstop who debuted professionally in 2001

Year	Age	Level	Games Played	Plate Appearances	At Bats	Batting Average	OBP	OPS
2001	18	Rookie/A Ball	69	288	262	.317	.365	.443
2002	19	Low-A/A Ball	127	539	486	.214	.270	.296
2003	20	High-A Ball	107	420	380	.211	.257	.295
2004	21	AA	116	432	384	.279	.328	.401
2005	22	AAA	65	275	245	.355	.403	.518

You may have guessed correctly that timing was the biggest difference in these two players' careers. Cedeño was simply in the better situation at the time he hit his stride. Cedeño began 2005 in Triple-A but was called up by the Cubs when Nomar Garciaparra went down with an injury. After making his debut on April 23, he appeared in just ten games, going 5-for-16 before being sent back down in favor of Neifi Perez and Enrique Wilson, who shared the shortstop duties during Garciaparra's extended absence.

Due to the Cubs' lack of stability at shortstop, Cedeño was given another chance at the major-league level. He was called up again in 2005 and stayed on the major-league roster through the end of the season, going 19-for-64 (.297) and driving in just four runs in several months. Chicago lacked a shortstop and so, Cedeño, who had hit .214 in A-ball and then .211 in High-A just three and four years ago, respectively, was the team's Opening Day starter in 2006.

Meanwhile, one season before Lambin's breakout campaign of 2005, another third baseman made his MLB debut with the Mets. His name was David Wright. Lambin, however, could also play shortstop. Unfortunately for him, Jose Reyes made his debut in 2003 and wasn't moving anytime soon. Despite these odds, Lambin thought his 2005 season was going to earn him a call-up, even if only in September.

"I really thought that was the year. . . . I thought, 'I'm going to get called up in September,' as a best-case scenario," Lambin said. "As a worst-case scenario, they'll put me on the 40-man roster in the offseason. If they don't put me on the 40-man, I'll at least have a big-league invite

Table I.2. Player B: Third baseman who debuted professionally in 2002

Year	Age	Level	Games Played	Plate Appearances	At Bats	Batting Average	OBP	OPS
2002	22	Low-A	47	192	179	.279	.316	.447
2003	23	High-A	118	459	401	.289	.366	.404
2004	24	AA	121	467	410	.244	.331	.390
2005	25	AA/AAA	114	440	392	.309	.372	.587

the next spring to show what I can do. . . . None of those things happened."

Lambin recognized himself as a fringe talent: capable of reaching the big leagues, but never of being an everyday player. With the Mets, though, it was clear even without Wright or Reyes, the team was going to fill its needs with established MLB players rather than with fringe players like Lambin.

"That was the turning point in my career where I was in my prime, I was productive, I was really, really good and the timing just didn't line up," Lambin said. "The Mets had the highest payroll in baseball. It wasn't the organization to get an opportunity with no matter what you were doing in the minor leagues. They were going to buy whatever they needed."

The Cubs at that time, on the other hand, were the perfect franchise for a middle infielder looking to get his shot. Cedeño got a lot of playing time as a result, and despite the fact he was worse than a replacement-level player, he suited up for seven different major-league teams in ten major-league seasons. The Cubs, Mariners, Pirates, Astros, Padres, Phillies, and eventually even the Mets all gave Cedeño the chance to play in the major leagues.

Cedeño's career slash line in the major leagues was .245/.289/.353. To call that line anemic would be generous. In his MLB career, Cedeño's cumulative WAR was −1.4. In other words, a "replacement-level" minor-league player would have been worth 1.4 more wins than Cedeño was over the course of his career. Simply by getting a chance to show himself to other teams in a big-league uniform, though, Cedeño was able to stay in the big leagues for a decade.

There was another player that came nearly 50 years before Lambin or Cedeño, who seemed destined for a longer-than-ten-year stay in the major leagues. As we've seen, though, timing and health can help make or break a major-league career.

Timing doesn't always have to do with opportunity or organizational depth: one poorly timed injury right as you're reaching your prime can derail your career. That was the unfortunate case for John Paciorek, who is widely regarded as the best cup of coffee player of all time.

At just 18 years old, Paciorek made his major-league debut for Houston on September 29, 1963, the final game of the season between the Colt .45's and the New York Mets. He was one of eight rookies starting for Houston that day. Within hours, he was easily the highlight of the season's curtain call, especially since the victorious Colt .45's finished 66–96 on the season and the Mets fell to 51–111 on the year, which is still one of the worst seasons in baseball history.

Paciorek appeared at the plate five times. He went 3-for-3 and walked twice. His three singles drove in three runs and he himself scored four times. He was about as productive as one can be while playing in just one major-league game. Fewer than 4,000 people got to see this teenage slugger's historic performance.[20] Still, there were thousands more eager Colt .45 fans—as well as fans from his hometown of Detroit—who were looking forward to bigger and better things from him.

The *Detroit Free Press* ran a story after the game with the headline "'Dream' Start for John" whose lede read:

> HOUSTON—Eighteen-year-old John Paciorek made his major league debut Sunday for the Houston Colts and the Hamtramck St. Ladislaus product showed every indication that he will be worth the $75,000 the Houston Colt .45's paid him to sign.[21]

He absolutely did show every indication he would be worth that signing bonus down to the penny. As Baseball Almanac points out in its summary of Paciorek's career, he started his 1964 campaign red hot as well. After he hit a bases-loaded triple against the Mets in a spring training game in late March, the *Ocala Star-Banner* ran a story jokingly stating, "The New York Mets may file an unfair child labor charge against the Houston Colts if young John Paciorek continues harassing them."[22] He wouldn't get the chance to harass them again.

Before the 1964 season began, with nothing but promise for his professional future, Paciorek suffered a serious back injury that required surgery and forced him to miss the rest of the 1964 season and all of

1965. After two years away from the game, he was an entirely different player. He held on and kept trying to make it back to the big leagues, but by the 1970s, he was finished with Organized Baseball entirely.[23]

Once again, timing was crucial. Had Paciorek not suffered that back injury, who is to say he wouldn't have become a superstar in the big leagues during the 1960s and '70s? At the same time, who's to say a couple of performances against a really bad Mets team didn't lead people into thinking he was destined for a decades-long career? There is, of course, no way to know for sure. That is what can ultimately eat away at a cup of coffee player: Is it better to have tasted the game's highest level just once, or to have never tasted it at all?

A look into the psyche of Olympic athletes lends some perspective on this very question. It is said that bronze medalists are most often actually happier than silver medalists. This is a result of counterfactual thinking, according to Peter McGraw, behavioral scientist at the University of Colorado, Boulder.[24] What he means is people tend to compare themselves to what could have been rather than their overall result. Logic would tell us a silver medalist would be happier, because they finished ahead of the bronze medalist, but this is not the case. A silver medalist can't stop thinking about what they could have done differently to win gold. Meanwhile, a bronze medalist is just happy to be standing on the podium.

Chase Lambin is the baseball equivalent of a bronze medalist. Would he have liked to reach the major leagues? Of course. But had he gotten there and not stuck, who's to say he would be happier for it in the long run?

There is another player like this, who gets his own story told later on. Ron Wright also suffered a back injury right as he was ready to take off as a right-handed power hitter. Unlike Paciorek, Wright hadn't made his major-league debut when he suffered his injury.

His one-game story is completely different from Paciorek's: instead of being a story of tragedy, in which a player's potential is undercut, Wright's is a story of the perseverance of a player who, in the face of adversity, was still able to reach his big-league dream. It only lasted a day, but in his case, it was about the journey, not the destination.

Chase Lambin, however, never got that day. He played 11 seasons in the minor leagues and two seasons in the Independent League. Now a coach for the Spokane Indians, the Texas Rangers' Class-A short-season team, Lambin preaches mental toughness to his players. He said if he hadn't had that, he wouldn't have lasted in the minor leagues nearly as long as he did.

"I guess with baseball, I was like Peter Pan. You just continue to kick that can down the road," Lambin said.

He also said the single-mindedness needed to succeed in baseball is unlike anything else in life. The player who starts considering options outside of baseball is already done. The deck gets stacked against him even more than it already was.

"The difference between the guys who make it and the guys who don't is mental," Lambin said. "The guy who is all in with no backup plan and has burned the boat is going to be better than the guy who's kicking around the idea in his head about selling insurance."

That is what makes reaching the major leagues so difficult. How do you look at your slim odds of reaching the big leagues and continue to believe in yourself? How do you continue to convince a partner to keep moving around the country in the hopes that, one day, it will all be worth it? For some, it becomes too much. For others, nothing they do on the field ever ends up being enough.

Even after being called up, some players perform admirably and are never given another chance. Chris Saenz made his major-league debut on April 24, 2004, for the Milwaukee Brewers against the St. Louis Cardinals. By most statistical measures, he pitched the best cup of coffee game in MLB history.

Facing a Cardinals lineup that would eventually reach the World Series and lose to the Red Sox, he went six innings, striking out seven, allowing just two hits, and zero runs on 93 pitches while earning the win.[25] Saenz is the only pitcher since 1899 to pitch in just one game and pitch at least six shutout innings.[26] At one point, Saenz set down 14 straight Cardinal hitters.

Saenz wasn't a random journeyman when he made this dominant start; he was 22 years old, and seemingly entering his prime. In the case of Saenz, timing worked both for and against him. Brewers starter Chris Capuano was injured, requiring the Brew Crew to call up a minor leaguer for a spot start. Saenz, previously in Double-A, was tabbed for the job.

Thus, thanks to the timing of an injury within the organization, Saenz got the opportunity to pitch in the big leagues and dominate a lineup that would win the National League pennant that same season. Ironically, it was thanks to the timing of his own injury that he never got back to the big leagues.

Once Capuano returned, Saenz was sent back down, and later that year he threw out his elbow, requiring him to get Tommy John surgery. He had to miss the entire 2005 and 2006 seasons and was never the same. An injury helped get him his first big-league opportunity, and an injury later ensured he would never get another one.

Injuries can take a career out of an athlete's control. For the majority of ballplayers, though, the difference between having a shot at the big leagues or not rests entirely in their own hands. Emotion control and mind-set are two of the most important components to a player's quest to make the major leagues. While perfectly calibrating your emotions and placing yourself in an ideal mind-set doesn't guarantee you a shot at the big leagues, those who study sports psychology seem to think it increases your chances.

Sports psychology consultant Robert Andrews, who works with Olympians like Simone Biles as well as baseball players, said while baseball is a very mental game, it's not as simple as closing one's mind off to the outside world.

"The word I use is 'balance.' If you just focus solely on baseball and nothing else in your life, then you're out of balance and you're going to be burned out," Andrews said. "Learning how to balance all that is a mark of strong ego and maturity, but you do have to be 'all in' to keep the dream alive."[27]

That dream is alive for everyone at a young age. Slowly, for most, that dream starts to die. For nearly all, the grind is too much.

"Nine out of ten guys would get crushed by the constant adversity the game brought," Chase Lambin said. "You add to that the injustices or the politics, it'll wear you down to a nub to where you lose that kid's spark. You lose that love for the game and the desire to put in the work."

Lambin talked about winning what he calls "the invisible battle." The invisible battle is between a hitter and a pitcher, and who wins depends on who trusts his own preparation, talent, and mind-set more. In many cases, if you win the invisible battle, you win the physical battle.

This battle goes beyond the physical, though. There is an invisible battle going on in each minor leaguer's head as he strives for his major-league dream. The battle these players go through on a daily basis is, naturally, mostly unseen: most play in front of small crowds for little more than peanuts. What these players go through on their way to the major leagues goes nearly unnoticed by anyone outside of themselves.

Each player in this book won his invisible battle and achieved his big-league dream, even if only for a moment. For these select few, the battle doesn't end after that one day in the big leagues. For the players with the distinguished honor of one game of MLB experience, the fight still rages on across the battlefield of the memory. Players whose debuts were made a decade or more ago still struggle with internal questions: Was all the hard work worth one day on a major-league field? Some are more at peace with the way their careers turned out than others.

Questions like this are hypothetical rather than literal for Lambin, who never got to live the major-league dream, even for a day. Now, Lambin says he's fine with the way his career played out. During his playing career, though, he would have given anything to get that one taste of the bigs.

"At the time, I would have given a lot. I might have given a finger, or a body part, or a lot of money," Lambin said. "But the further I get from playing, the more grateful I am that it didn't happen, because I almost wear it as a badge of honor. . . . Maybe if I had gotten that one day, I wouldn't have been satisfied or it wouldn't have lived up to my expectations. Maybe it would have been great. I'll never know."

Robert Andrews also hypothesized what the mental toll might be on a player who got just one game in the major leagues.

"If you've ever had a dream where it's just an amazing dream and it's awesome and you're so excited and happy in this dream and then you wake up and realize it was a dream and it's over," Andrews said, "you have to deal with that and seeing that begin to fade away is almost like you drive by, see it and you look at it, but then it passes and it's over. . . . Having that one shot at the majors and it's fleeting and then it's gone, I would think that would be really hard to deal with."

Each player in this book won his first invisible battle: reaching the big leagues. Now, unlike almost any other player in big-league history, each faces a second battle, unseen by everyone else: If you could go back to when you were a boy, would you still say reaching the major leagues was your dream?

That is the question at the heart of this book. It is a question asked of a player whose teammates had to get his manager to play him before he got sent back down. It is a question posed to a player whose once-promising career was cut short by a doctor's surgical mistake.

A player whose drug and alcohol abuse got in the way of a promising major-league career is asked this question. The pitcher who never latched onto the right team at the right time is asked this question.

We ask this question of a Hall of Famer's brother whose only career major-league game was the only game he and his famous sibling ever played on the same field. The former major-league manager who used his experience to shape current big leaguers is asked this question. We even ask this question of the player whose dad is in the Hall of Fame, but who couldn't find the same love for professional baseball 60 years ago.

So now, the question goes back to you: What would you give to make your childhood dream a reality? Would you be willing to face the "invisible battle" knowing there's a chance you may have to face another after your career has run its course?

For the players in this book, whose stories are told in their own words, their second "invisible battle," now as retired ballplayers, is well under way. Unlike the countless battles they went through on their way to "The Show," the doubt, joy, internal questions, and uncertainty accompanying these battles aren't invisible anymore.

CHARLIE LINDSTROM

September 28, 1958

A longtime New York Giants outfielder, 1936 Brooklyn Dodgers utility man Freddie Lindstrom walked away from the game that made him famous on May 15, 1936, 12 years after his career began.[1] Lindstrom, just 30 years old after starting his baseball career fresh out of high school, had a wife roughly halfway through her pregnancy with their third son; his playing days were behind him. Thirty-nine years later, Lindstrom, a career .311 hitter, would be voted into the National Baseball Hall of Fame. He retired just four months before his youngest son, Charlie, was born.

On September 7, 1936, Charlie "Chuck" Lindstrom was welcomed into the world.[2] His older brother Fred was already showing the makings of a future athlete, and everything pointed to Charlie being raised by a family full of them.

Like his brothers and parents, Charlie was born on the South Side of Chicago in White Sox country. That's where he called home until grade school when his parents moved north to Evanston, home of Northwestern University, the "Harvard of the Midwest." While growing up, he could already see his brother Fred playing in the shadow of his father, a recently retired star baseball player.

"The one who had the most difficult time making the adjustment was my brother, Fred," Lindstrom said. "All the newspaper articles always started out with 'Son of Freddie Lindstrom, blah, blah, blah.'"

Charlie was six years younger and thus more removed from his dad's playing career by the time he was starring for New Trier High School in only his sophomore year. This worked in Charlie's favor, as he had a less difficult time bearing the weight that came with his family name.

"It was one of those things that if you're around them all the time, you don't think that much of it. He's just your dad," Lindstrom said. "By the

Charlie Lindstrom takes fielding practice for the White Sox during the 1958 season. *Courtesy of the Lindstrom Family Collection*

time it got to me, nobody was interested in it anyhow. It was still there, but it wasn't as big of a deal."

Living in the extant shadow of his father didn't stop Charlie from being the catcher for some very successful teams in high school and summer ball. His New Trier baseball teams finished state runners up two of his three seasons there (he transferred after his freshman year at Loyola). Now 82, the light, lachrymose "what if" in his voice was still clear as he vividly recalled memories from nearly 70 years prior.

"We came in second two years out of the three I was there," Lindstrom said. "We lost the championship game both of those years: one to Springfield and the next year to Belleville."

Charlie, along with many of his New Trier teammates, also represented Winnetka Post American Legion during the summers and even found success at the national level. Again, Lindstrom's memory shoots right back to the summers; though they filled his adolescence with joy, he associated his time on the actual ball field with heartbreak.

"We went on to lose the championship game of the American Legion World Series down in Miami," Lindstrom said. "We won 30 games and we lost two and the only team to beat us was from Yakima, Washington. They beat us twice."

Despite not winning the national championship, people around the country were noticing Lindstrom's baseball talent. He was named the American Legion "Player of the Year" in 1953 and was gaining notoriety among Division I college coaches nationwide.[3] He garnered offers from such schools as UCLA and USC, but Lindstrom was a Chicago man through and through and didn't want to make the seven- or eight-hour plane ride (air travel was far from perfected by 1953) to the West Coast.

"Those schools had very good programs, very good coaches and they were very nice to extend the offers to me," Lindstrom said. "In the end, I just said, 'I think I'll stay closer to home.'"

That's exactly what Lindstrom did, deciding to play at Northwestern, where his dad had become the baseball coach. Despite getting scholarship offers from some of the most elite institutions in the country, Lindstrom wasn't really interested in a postsecondary education. He wanted to be like his dad and go to the big leagues right out of high school.

"The last thing in the world I wanted to do was go to college," Lindstrom said. "I didn't like school; I never liked school, so the thought of going to school, no matter where it was, was not very appealing. . . . At that time, I wanted to play professional baseball, but nobody came knocking on my door, so I was somewhat disappointed."

He was also disappointed in his fraternity's food from time to time. Luckily for him, his fraternity house was only seven miles from his childhood home.

"When the food got too bad at the fraternity house, I would go home for a while," Lindstrom said. "The food was definitely better at home."

After three years of doing that at Northwestern, he did something that would enable him to put food on the table himself: on June 17, 1957, he signed with his South Side Chicago White Sox. He remembers his signing bonus being $6,500.

He had made even more of a name for himself playing for a summer ball team in Watertown, South Dakota, in the Basin League. Among his teammates were Dick Howser, future New York Yankees manager; Norm Stewart, future legendary University of Missouri basketball coach; and Ron Perranoski. Perranoski was traded by the Cubs for Don Zimmer,[4] recorded a save for the Los Angeles Dodgers in the 1963 World Series,[5] which they won in four games, and served as LA's pitching coach from 1981 to 1994.[6] He won two rings as a player, two as a coach with the Dodgers.

During that summer baseball season, before he was playing professionally, Lindstrom could already see the lifestyle of a pro ballplayer might not be his cup of tea.

"We traveled a lot for that team and I didn't like that every single day of your life was putting on a baseball uniform and doing your thing," Lindstrom said. "I enjoyed it when we were in high school, I enjoyed it when we were in college, but when you're playing 165 games a year, it wears on you."

Nonetheless, it had been his dream to play professional baseball, and that dream was realized when he inked his deal with the White Sox in 1957. He reported to the Colorado Springs Sky Sox as a 20-year-old looking to prove himself. In 66 games there, he hit just .222 with four home runs. It was in the following year that he would break out.

In 1958, his first full season in professional baseball, Lindstrom reported to the Davenport DavSox of the Three-I League. He played against guys like Boog Powell, who went on to win two World Series and the 1970 American League MVP Award and hit 339 big-league home runs, mostly with the Baltimore Orioles. He also played with Dean Chance,

1964 American League Cy Young winner for the Los Angeles Angels. Frank Howard was also in that league at the time; he won the 1960 Rookie of the Year Award and, along with Perranoski, won a World Series with the Dodgers in 1963.

Even with such future big names, only two players to that point were named unanimously to the Three-I All-Star team, according to Charlie. He was one of them. Another catcher playing against Lindstrom was one who is most remembered for his work in the press box rather than the catcher's box: Bob Uecker played in the league before reaching the major leagues and eventually becoming one of the most notable play-by-play announcers in baseball history.[7]

In 1958 for the blandly named "DavSox," Lindstrom came into his own, posting a .276/.342/.434 slash line with 14 home runs. As Lindstrom recalled, in those days, if a player signed for more than $4,500 (which Lindstrom did), they were expected to be on the big-league ball club after completing their first full minor-league season.

"I knew at the end of the year, wherever I was playing, if the White Sox were still playing, they were paying me, so I'd go to Chicago," Lindstrom said. "I would catch batting practice or something."

He ended up getting to do more than just catch batting practice. As soon as the DavSox' season came to an end, Lindstrom reported to the White Sox. With about a dozen games left, he sat on the bench through the first 11. It wasn't until the final day of the 1958 regular season that Lindstrom got his shot.

"The manager, Al Lopez, told me I was going to catch in our last game," Lindstrom said. "I thought, 'Fine, this is good.'"

The ever-understated Lindstrom was disappointed when he arrived at Comiskey Park and read down the lineup card for the final game of the season against the Kansas City Athletics.

"We got to the ballpark and the lineup cards were out and John Romano was the catcher instead of me," Lindstrom said. He added nonchalantly, "I went, 'Well, that's life.'"

With nothing left to do but watch his team's final contest of the season, Lindstrom had to accept the possibility that he would go his entire 1958 major-league stint without taking the field. That is, however, until the fifth inning when Lindstrom was installed at catcher in relief of Romano.

It was his first major-league appearance and right down the road from where most of his family was from on the South Side of Chicago. With one man on and two outs in the top of the fifth, Roger Maris was batting for the Athletics. He would become baseball's new home run king while wearing Yankees pinstripes just three years later. With Maris batting, Lindstrom gave up a passed ball, allowing a runner to move into scoring position. Luckily for him, the run didn't score.

His first career plate appearance came in the bottom of the sixth against Bob Davis. He drew a leadoff walk and came around to score when Don Mueller singled to left field later in the inning. It was a relatively mundane, albeit productive start to a major-league career. It was befitting of the atmosphere that Lindstrom recalled from the small crowd of 4,000 people who were there that day.[8]

"You have a season that starts in spring training in February and you play every day, so by the time you get to the last game of the season, nobody is particularly pumped up," Lindstrom said.

At least a few people rose to their feet the second time Lindstrom came up, though. He stepped into the box in the bottom of the seventh with two outs and a 7–4 lead, Johnny Callison on first base. He struck the second pitch he saw cleanly to the opposite field and was off to the races.

"I hit the ball off the top of the right-center-field fence and got a triple," Lindstrom said. "That's the only time I've ever been at bat in the big leagues."

Lindstrom quickly pointed out his career 1.000 batting average and 3.000 slugging percentage. They are feats that are, ironically, only possible due to the brevity of what seemed like a promising big-league career. Even while standing on third, Lindstrom didn't think much of what he'd just done.

"I got to third base and it was no big deal," Lindstrom said. "I had hit many triples in my life, because I was known for my great speed, but if I was only going to have one hit, it might as well be unique. . . . That is my unique mark on baseball. I didn't think much of it, because I was still very confident I would play a lot more baseball in my remaining years, but that never materialized."

The White Sox won the game 11–4 and finished the season 82–72. After making his major-league debut and recording his first big-league hit, his parents greeted him after the game and celebrated the culmination of what he had worked for in his life to that point. The evening that followed Charlie's performance seemed inconsequential, almost a lost memory. Many cup of coffee guys have come to know these moments too well: the significance of one moment in a lifetime can only be put into proper perspective once an entire career has played out. The Sox finale that season would be his only shot; perhaps he would have celebrated differently had he known.

"After the game, my mom and dad were there, and I remember to this day, my mom was by far the most thrilled and we went out and had a nice steak dinner that night and she was just thrilled to death," Lindstrom said. "I wasn't particularly thrilled, because I thought there would be many more opportunities as time went on, but that didn't happen."

As the struggle wore on, Lindstrom's distaste for the life of a professional ballplayer started to become more and more apparent, especially as he was seemingly passed over for opportunities. He described his own 1959 spring training campaign as "very good," and he expected to be sent to the Triple-A club in Indianapolis. Instead, he was sent to Charleston, South Carolina, to play A-ball in the Sally League.

Had Lindstrom gone to Triple-A and proven worthy of a spot on the White Sox's major-league roster that season, he would have become part of one of the most famous South Side teams of all time. His timing was nearly perfect, but he wasn't able to be a part of that legendary White Sox team.

The 1959 Chicago White Sox were known affectionately by their fans as the "Go-Go White Sox" based on their scrappy play. A song, "Go, Go-Go White Sox," was written by former Sox minor leaguer Al Trace and his friend Walter Jagiello. It was the rallying cry for a season that would go down in White Sox lore. The South Siders won the American League pennant, going 94–60, punching their ticket to the World Series for the first time since the infamous 1919 "Black Sox" scandal. Ultimately, they lost to the Dodgers, who were in just their second season in Los Angeles.[9]

Chicago brought back the song midway through the 2005 season for a throwback night against those same Dodgers. Coincidentally or not, the White Sox went on to win the 2005 World Series, breaking an 88-year championship drought. Perhaps, if the baseball life were more fit for Lindstrom, he would have been a part of that 1959 team that continues to endure with White Sox fans to this day.

"In those days, you had to be a dedicated ballplayer. That was the dominant thing you did in your life and there were things that happened that I didn't understand," Lindstrom said. "I really wasn't a tough enough mental athlete to accept those things. I probably would have been successful except I wasn't any good at adjusting to the baseball life."

He felt so out of place and so dejected after a 1959 season where he hit .219 with just four home runs in the Sally League, he thought it might be time to call it a career.

"It was long traveling and I didn't enjoy it, so I said, 'Wait a minute, I've put in my time. I've shown them I can be successful and here I am three leagues down from where I want to be and I really don't feel like doing this for five years until I get my chance,'" Lindstrom said. "If they don't want to give me the chance, that's fine. So, I left. I quit."

Lindstrom's retirement was short lived as he eventually returned the following season with hopes that MLB expansion might help him land a job somewhere else. When he returned, he was reminded of why he left in the first place.

"We were sent down to Hollywood, Florida, for minor-league spring training and we had a great big empty lot next to the railroad tracks and they had a chain-link backstop in one corner and another one diagonally across the field from it," Lindstrom said.

"We had five or six minor-league teams that were in Hollywood and when we would take batting practice, we would take it on both corners of the field. Our outfielders would have their backs turned to balls being hit at them from the other direction."

An optimistic picture of the onset of the season this does not paint.

As it turned out, it was that 1960 season in which Lindstrom realized he did not have the burning passion for baseball necessary to succeed at its highest level. While playing for the Lincoln Chiefs of the Three-I League, he struck up a conversation with relief pitcher and fellow Chicagoland ballplayer Dan Osinski, who grew up in Barrington, Illinois. Osinski had done a significant stretch in the minors himself by this time, and Lindstrom had the sense he wasn't cut out to do the same.

"I said to him, 'Dan, am I correct: You've been playing minor-league baseball for seven years?' He said, 'Yep,' and I go, 'You've got to be kidding me,'" Lindstrom said.

Osinski began his playing career at the age of 18 in 1952 and was out of Organized Baseball in 1957 and 1958, so by the time he had this conversation with Lindstrom, he'd been in or around Organized Baseball for nearly a decade. Yet he still had not appeared in a major-league game.

Lindstrom recalled Osinski's thoughts: "Chuck, I'm a carpenter, and I can be a carpenter when I'm 50 years old, but as long as somebody will pay me to throw a baseball, I'm going to do that," the carpenter told the ballplayer. "I get tired of doing carpentry and baseball is what I would like to be able to do as long as there's a spot for me."

That sort of drive, self-awareness, and dedication makes a major-league competitor. To Lindstrom, hearing that from someone who still hadn't reached his dream was very powerful. It was at that moment that Lindstrom realized he didn't have the mental fortitude to carve out a long major-league career. To this day, Lindstrom can't believe how the rest of Osinski's career went: in 1962, ten years after he pitched in his first professional baseball game, he made his major-league debut for the Kansas City Athletics.

Osinski's mental fortitude was rewarded with a solid big-league career in which he went 29–28 with a 3.34 ERA. Six years after that conversation with Lindstrom, he was pitching in Game Seven of the World Series for the Boston Red Sox against the St. Louis Cardinals. Boston lost the game and the series, but Osinski got to pitch on the biggest stage in the world.

"To me, even for that to be my outcome, it wouldn't have been worth it," Lindstrom said.

Finishing the 1960 season in the Sally League with the Charleston ChaSox, Lindstrom averaged just .219 at the dish. The White Sox, having given up, sold his contract to the San Diego Padres. No, they weren't yet a major-league team; they were a Pacific Coast League team, equivalent to Triple-A. They were also the first team for whom Ted Williams played professional baseball; they were the first stop on the way to one of the game's greatest careers. For Lindstrom, however, this was not the first stop; it seemed it was merely the next one, as he received a formal offer from the Padres.

Their new general manager was Ralph Kiner, former Pirates star outfielder and now a Hall of Famer. Kiner sent Lindstrom a contract offer that he remembered being for one year, $3,500. According to Lindstrom, he had made $6,500 the previous season, so the offer was insulting. He wrote back to Kiner asking him to reconsider and make a more reasonable offer.

"The next week, I got a letter back and it said, 'This is what our offer is,'" Lindstrom recalled.

The stark realization set in: this was not a negotiation. The $3,500 contract offer was all that was on the table for Lindstrom, so he decided to get creative. He proposed that he receive a one-year contract at the rate he had made in 1960 if he made the Triple-A club, but would accept the reduced-pay contract if he wasn't able to make the team and was sent to the Sally League or somewhere else.

"I remember his response very well," Lindstrom said. "He wrote back, 'I have wasted two three-cent stamps on you so far. If you don't care to sign this contract, I'm not going to waste a third.'" Well, there you go.

At this point, for the second time in his career, Lindstrom briefly decided that would be the end of his professional baseball career. Just as he did the first time, he quickly changed his mind.

"By the time spring training came around, I said, 'Well, if they want to give me a shot, I'll sign,'" Lindstrom said. Even in a less-than-ideal situation, a man who has given everything for the chance to keep playing baseball will take another chance to suit up.

He signed and reported to San Diego's spring training facility in Palm Springs, California. He finished spring training there and was given a contract to go back to Hollywood, Florida, where the White Sox's lower minor-league spring training was held.

"Once I found out where I was going, that night I went up and had three or four creme de menthes," Lindstrom said. "When I woke up, I felt like the dickens."

The rest of the day did nothing to cure his hangover. Lindstrom boarded a small plane in Palm Springs en route to Los Angeles where he would catch a connecting flight to Miami.

"The plane was wobbling all over the place, I broke out in a sweat. I was miserable," Lindstrom said. "There was a horseshoe seating arrangement and I was sitting in the back of the plane, my shirt is soaking wet, I feel horrible, and some guy tapped me on the shoulder and goes, 'Hey aren't you Chuck Lindstrom?' . . . I didn't want to see anybody or anybody to know who I was on that flight."

A turbulent plane ride with a hangover has a way of inspiring decisions upon landing. For Chuck Lindstrom, that flight to Los Angeles was a wake-up call. He never boarded his plane to Miami.

"I got to the airport in Los Angeles and I cashed in my ticket to Miami and exchanged it and flew back to Chicago instead and said, 'This is the end,'" he recalled.

Of course, for the third time, Lindstrom ended up giving it one more shot. He played less than half a season for the Chiefs in the Three-I League during the 1961 season while batting just .197. During the season, he accepted a coaching and teaching position at Lincoln College in Lincoln, Illinois. It was in Lincoln, Nebraska, however, that his most memorable moment in professional baseball occurred.

He had informed the Chiefs of his teaching and coaching job at Lincoln College and told them he would be leaving before the season ended. Therefore, he knew when his final game would be. On the day of that game, for the final time, he walked from the on-deck circle, giving his career a sense of the closure that many aspiring ballplayers never feel.

"I got in the batter's box and thought, 'This will be the last time I'm ever going to bat in Organized Baseball,'" Lindstrom recalled realizing. "Lincoln, Nebraska, had a big ballpark and they had a scoreboard in left-center field; I had not hit a home run at home or really come close all year long. . . . I said to myself, 'This is the last time,' and when the ball came in, I hit it over the scoreboard." The triumph of that moment lent some validation to all of the self-imposed suffering and labor that came to define Chuck Lindstrom's time as a professional ballplayer.

It was quite the way for his short-lived baseball career to come to a close, and it put a bow on a career Lindstrom didn't seem too keen on continuing anyway. He rounded third base, and his teammates in the bullpen teased him, saying the home run would convince him, once again, that he should keep playing. Lindstrom wasn't having any of that. The big moment helped him more perfectly sum up his life in professional baseball.

"I always said my career was outstanding in the very beginning and outstanding in the very end and left something to be desired between the two," Lindstrom said.

When he finished high school, after garnering no major-league interest, Lindstrom had expressed his disappointment to his dad, who never attended college. His playing career now over, his father informed him that he had, in fact, attracted interest from teams. His dad fielded the calls and didn't complete the relay throw to Chuck.

"He told me, 'Chuck, you had an opportunity. I had a number of clubs who got in touch with me and I told them I wanted you to get an education before going into baseball,'" Lindstrom recalled. To some, this may seem like a betrayal, but Chuck didn't see it that way.

"That was the most important decision my dad ever made, because the truth of the matter is once I got into professional baseball, I really didn't like it that well."

Had Freddie Lindstrom let his son follow his dream of playing professional baseball before going to college, his career may have fizzled out just the same and without him receiving three years of education from one of the top universities in the country. It helped set Chuck up for what was next in life at Lincoln College and beyond.

"When my dad left Loyola [high school], he burned all of his bridges. He didn't have any other options," Lindstrom explained. "He made up his mind there weren't going to be any of the obstacles that were going to bother him. . . . Those obstacles did bother me, because I had graduated from New Trier, a very good high school, and I had gone to three years at Northwestern. I had a different perspective on things than my dad."

Chuck took over as Lincoln College's baseball coach and eventually as the school's athletic director. He spent 23 years building a very good program. Many of his most lasting friendships, Lindstrom said, were forged at Lincoln College. During his tenure as athletic director, the school expanded from four to ten competitive team sports. His contributions to the school as a baseball coach and athletic director earned him honorary alumnus status in 2009.[10]

During Lincoln's 2013 homecoming, he became a member of the school's inaugural Hall of Fame class honoring "student-athletes, teams, coaches, managers, administrators, faculty, staff, and friends who have distinguished themselves in the field of athletics at Lincoln College."

Once Lindstrom's time at Lincoln was up in 1983, he went into the lighting business, joining Musco Lighting for a short time. He eventually returned to serve Lincoln once more, this time as its park director. When he became park director, he also started his own lighting business, something that likely wouldn't have been possible if his father had allowed him to enter professional baseball without a college education.

His company, Universal Sports Lighting, which he sold in 2014 upon retirement, has installed lights at ballparks around the country. According to Lindstrom, they've installed the lights at spring training sites in Surprise, Arizona, the University of San Diego, Princeton, and the U.S. Naval Academy, to name a few. It has allowed Lindstrom to stay connected to the baseball community without playing or coaching.

"I was affiliated with Major League Baseball and would go to the winter meetings and stuff like that thanks to my business," Lindstrom said. "I stayed in touch with the baseball world primarily through my business rather than through my baseball experience."

Lindstrom doesn't look back on his one game very much other than to appreciate the novelty of it, and the fact that he is one of the most accomplished one-game hitters ever. Given his lack of enthusiasm toward the daily grind of professional baseball, that shouldn't be surprising.

Just because he didn't particularly enjoy the life of professional baseball, though, doesn't mean he didn't leave a lasting impact on it. Blocks from where he was born, and where most of his family grew up on the South Side of Chicago, the lights beam down on the White Sox's Guaranteed Rate Field.

In the parking lot of old Comiskey Park where Lindstrom walked and hit a triple on September 28, 1958, stands the White Sox's current stadium. The lights that make night games possible in the modern day were installed by Lindstrom's company, ensuring Chuck Lindstrom's long, convoluted, and unlikely connection to baseball continues mere blocks from where it began.

2

ROE SKIDMORE

September 17, 1970

Every Saturday morning, as the sun rose over Decatur, Illinois, a young Roe Skidmore and his pals would run over to a local park to stake out their spot. If they wanted to play baseball that day, they had to get the perfect patch of grass. Not far from the park in the 1950s was the home of the Decatur Commodores, an A-ball club of which Skidmore was an avid fan.

"My dad would come home at five o'clock," Skidmore said. "We'd eat supper real quick and when the Commodores were in town, we'd load up the car and go watch the Commodores play."

Robert Skidmore would never go by "Bob," "Bobby," "Rob," or "Robbie"; from the time he was in grade school, he went by "Roe," his father's name. It allowed him to emulate his dad, a shoe salesman. It also endowed him with a name that sounded like it was made for the big leagues. "Roe Skidmore" sounds like it was taken right from a rookie card in a trading deck. From the time he was young, that's all he can remember wanting to be.

"In about the eighth inning of Commodores games, I'd be pulling on my dad's pants asking him if we could go by the tunnel so we could watch them walk by," Skidmore said. "That was an even bigger deal than watching them play. . . . I thought, 'Boy, if I could ever be one of those guys.'"

If you live in Decatur, which is actually slightly closer to St. Louis than it is to Chicago, you only have two options of which major-league team you can root for: the Cardinals or the Cubs.

"You can take two steps and there are Cubs fans, you take two more steps and there are Cardinals fans," Skidmore said. "It's pretty well split."

Like so many baseball fans before him, his dad played an important role in determining where his allegiances would lie. The elder Roe would come home from work, sit in his chair, and turn on two radios, each sitting side by side. One was tuned to the Cubs game so he could root for the North Siders, the other was tuned to the Cardinals game, broadcast by Harry Caray, so he could root against the Redbirds with vitriol.

His father's intense love for the game, and hatred for the Cardinals, helped fuel Roe toward playing baseball at a high level. At times, he could be obsessive. Fortunately, that obsession was tolerated by his supportive parents.

"I used to pound the rubber ball against the foundation of the house by the hour and they never said a word," Skidmore said. "I'm not sure my mom really liked that, but they let me do it."

As he grew older and stronger, baseball became as much a calling as it was a passion. The population of Decatur was between 70,000 and 80,000 during Roe's childhood,[1] and as it happened, three of them were professional scouts. It enabled Skidmore to get looks other prospects might not.

"They were always around at the park, and when I was in high school, they came to a lot of the games," Skidmore said. "The professional part of it was always in front of me. I was around it since I was a little kid."

The first scout was Richie Klaus, with the Giants organization. San Francisco had another scout, Gene "Swede" Thompson, who played six seasons for the Reds and Giants. He would have played more if he hadn't lost three years to military service in World War II. The third scout living in Decatur was Al Unser, for the Cleveland Indians.

Those scouts continued taking notice as Skidmore worked his way up at Eisenhower High School. His junior year, the team reached the state championship game to take on Morton, a Chicago-area powerhouse. In an epic upset, Skidmore's club, managed by Clete Hinton, won the state championship in 1962.[2] Hinton was a man most players looked up to and still keep in touch with to this day.

While Skidmore was talented, he wasn't talented enough to be drafted out of high school. He decided to attend Millikin University in Decatur,

Roe Skidmore poses for his wife, Jan, at Wrigley Field during the 1970 season.
Courtesy of Jan Skidmore

so the same scouts continued tracking his progress as the boy became a man on the baseball field. By 1966, he had done enough in college to convince himself he might get drafted by an MLB team.

The state baseball championship was being played in Peoria that summer, and Skidmore got a call from Unser, the former Indians scout who was now working for the Braves, playing their first season in Atlanta.

"Do you want to ride up to Peoria with me? I'm going to scout some guys up there during the high school finals," Unser asked Skidmore.

Skidmore obliged, and the pair drove the 80 miles northwest to Peoria to watch Illinois's best and brightest young ballplayers. They spent all day watching high school baseball games; then they made their way back. They arrived at Skidmore's house, and Unser asked if it was okay for him to come inside. He asked Skidmore if his dad was home. Skidmore responded that he was sure he was back from work by then. Once everyone sat down, Unser delivered the news.

"You didn't know it today, but the Braves are going to draft you and I'm going to pay you $2,500 if you'll sign," Unser told the Skidmores.

"Of course, $2,500 was probably $2,500 more than I had seen in the same place to that point in my life," Skidmore said, looking back on that day. At that moment, however, he wasn't thinking about the money.

"If I had any money, I would've paid them to be able to play."

Skidmore, a catcher and third baseman, was hardly a hot commodity; he was taken in the 47th round of the draft. Still, the Braves had made good on their word and selected him, giving him a shot to play professional baseball. Within a week, he had signed with the Braves and was headed to the West Coast.

"A week later, I was on a plane to Yakima, Washington, wherever that is," Skidmore said.

He was sent to the Yakima Braves, Atlanta's Low-A affiliate in the Northwest League. Getting sparing at bats and irregular playing time, Skidmore sputtered to a .193 batting average in 47 games.[3] It wasn't a desirable start to a professional baseball career.

In spring training the following year, Skidmore broke his ankle, keeping him on the shelf for several weeks. He came back with the West Palm Beach Braves, the team's Single-A affiliate. However, he played just nine games there before Atlanta decided to cut him loose.

"They should have, because I sure didn't show them anything," Skidmore said. "They figured I was a waste for them."

Returning to his pregnant wife, Skidmore, dejected, drove 22 hours straight through to Decatur. He went right to his dad's house to use the phone. Gene Thompson was the man he needed to call.

"Gene, I just got released by the Braves. Do you have any jobs in the Giants organization?" Skidmore asked the San Francisco scout.

"Hang in there. I'll call you right back," Thompson responded.

After a 30-minute wait that felt like a lifetime, Thompson called Skidmore back. He told Skidmore they had a rookie first baseman hitting .150 and they were going to send him back to rookie league. Then came the kicker.

"Have you ever played first base? I don't remember you playing first base," Thompson asked after laying out the situation.

"Oh yeah, I've played it off and on a lot," Skidmore responded. He had never played first base in his life. For another shot, though? He was sure he could figure it out.

Only one thing mattered to Roe: he could smell another job in professional baseball.

"Go out tomorrow and the general manager will sign you," Thompson instructed. "You have a doubleheader against Quincy."

Thus, Skidmore had the second chance he was looking for.

"I was almost done before I got started and Gene Thompson gave me another chance," Skidmore said. "If it hadn't been for him, I'd probably be loading boxes at UPS or something."

The Decatur Commodores were still in town, now the Giants' Single-A affiliate. Skidmore's second chance would come in his hometown, playing with the team he grew up watching. The earth on which he stood was, to him and his father, hallowed ground. None of that was on Skidmore's mind, though, as he prepared for his debut performance with the Commodores.

"The thing I most remember thinking is, 'Okay, buddy, this is your shot. You're getting another chance. You better not blow it this time,'" Skidmore said.

He didn't blow it. After being assured he was going to be the everyday first baseman for the Commodores, his nerves settled. He was able to just go up and hit.

And hit, he did.

Across the doubleheader against Quincy, which Skidmore vividly recounted, he went 6-for-7 with two home runs, one in each game of the double dip. In a matter of hours, he had established himself as the every-day first baseman for a Single-A club despite never playing the position before. It signaled the rebirth of his career. In a sense, it was the birth of a new ballplayer: Roe Skidmore, first baseman.

"I was so low driving back home just 24 hours earlier. I was lower than a snake," Skidmore said. "Then, that happened and, boy, I was floating again."

In 99 games with the Commodores in 1967, he hit .274 with 14 hom-ers and 67 RBIs. It represented a huge step up from his first go around professional baseball. It was clear he was a legitimate power threat. He followed that up by hitting .246 with 27 home runs and 94 RBIs in 117 games for the Commodores in 1968. During the Arizona Instructional League that winter, he continued to dazzle. He made many friends in the Cubs organization, a team whose players he often battled during that winter. He could tell Chicago liked him.

Skidmore returned to Decatur around Christmastime, shortly before 1969, and visited his dad at his shoe store. His father started in on him right away.

"A guy just came into the store and told me he saw in the paper somewhere that the Cubs had drafted you into their organization," the elder Roe said. "Do you know anything about this?"

Skidmore did not know what his dad was talking about. He had not been contacted by the Cubs. That did not, however, mean that the infor-mation coming from his father was inaccurate.

"That was news to me," Skidmore said. "I don't know when they were planning on letting me know, but I didn't know anything about it."

A couple of days later, the Cubs called Skidmore and confirmed the report they had taken him in the 1968 minor-league player draft, a precur-sor to the modern-day Rule 5 draft.[4] Having grown up a Cubs fan, Skid-more was now a member of the organization he'd rooted for his whole life. It was like the Commodores all over again, except this time it was the big-league team he'd always loved.

"My dad was more excited than I was," Skidmore said. "It was the Cubs. He went around town bragging and telling everybody about his kid being with the Cubs."

Logistically, the move was great for Skidmore too. Based on rules at the time, if a team drafted a player in the minor-league player draft, they had to play them a level above where they were listed on the other team's roster in order to keep them. Even though he hadn't played a game in Double-A yet, Skidmore was sitting serendipitously on San Francisco's Double-A roster when he was taken by the Cubs. That meant if he was to stick with the Cubs, he'd be playing in Triple-A, skipping right over Double-A.

Chicago was invested in Skidmore, whom they were more than willing to promote to Triple-A. Whitey Lockman was his manager at Triple-A Tacoma, and he sat him down to deliver an incredible vote of confidence.

"Listen, the reason the Cubs got you, is because Ernie Banks is going to be retiring after next season," Skidmore remembered Lockman telling him.

Once Banks, one of the greatest hitters of his generation, retired, his spot at first base had Skidmore's name on it. Bear in mind that Skidmore had about 70 total outings at first base under his belt. Now all of a sudden he was being groomed to replace "Mr. Cub." For many young players, especially for a lifelong Cubs fan, the news may have added pressure. Skidmore remembered the news actually taking the pressure off.

"That helped me mentally to know they were watching me and had their eye on me to take Ernie's place," Skidmore said. "It was just some confidence to know they drafted me with a purpose, for a specific reason."

Even the foul-mouthed Leo Durocher, who had taken the likes of Jackie Robinson and Willie Mays under his wing over the years, sang Skidmore's praises as a potential replacement for the greatest hitter in Cubs history.

Now playing in the Cubs organization, Skidmore put together a solid 1969 campaign in Tacoma. He hit .261 with 16 homers and 84 RBIs; he was the team's biggest power threat. The season was coming to a close when he and his teammate, pitcher Jim Dunegan, joined manager Whitey Lockman at an autograph signing at a local Sears store.

"We met Whitey at the store and we were sitting there signing autographs and Whitey Lockman goes, 'Oh, by the way, both of you are going to the big leagues after our last game,'" Skidmore said. "That's how I found out. It was very matter of fact, 'Oh, by the way. . .'" What to Lockman was a parenthetical afterthought, to Roe was the culminating sentence of a lifetime dream.

Skidmore, Dunegan, and company were cursed by their own success in 1969. They were the cream of the crop in the Pacific Coast League and ended up beating Eugene for the title. As a result, they played an extra week into the season.

"That was torture, because we knew we were going to get called up, but we obviously had to keep playing in the playoffs for the PCL," Skidmore remembered.

Finally, after winning a PCL title, Skidmore made his way to the big-league club, enjoying his first taste of the major leagues. However, this was the Cubs and the year was 1969. You know how this story ends. Durocher continued to play his same lineup day after day. Skidmore and the other rookies rode the bench.

"I had some good seats for the games the Cubs lost in September that year," Skidmore said. "It was pretty frustrating. You want to get in there and prove something."

He had an especially great seat for one of the lasting images of the Cubs' cursed days. On September 9, 1969, the Cubs were playing the Mets, a team that had trimmed a 9 1/2-game lead on August 15 into a 1 1/2-game lead for first place in the NL East entering play. Losers of five straight, the Cubs were in free fall. With Ron Santo on deck, a black cat raced from the stands onto the field at Shea Stadium in New York. Hiding from Durocher on the bench, Skidmore saw it all unfold.

"It was weird, because it really didn't run out onto the field, it was almost like it was trained," Skidmore remembered. "It was just running back and forth in front of the Cubs dugout, which was really the point, right?" It was an ominous scene, and Skidmore would become an immortal part of it in the lasting photograph of the moment, frozen in time.

"It's an infamous way to be in a picture. I was sitting right on the bench."

Skidmore got to see that and other games as the Cubs collapsed down the stretch, yielding the division to the "Miracle" Mets. As Chicago slowly gave away its lead, the mood in the locker room got more and more tense.

"One of the things the current Cubs are experiencing with Joe Maddon is that he's very intent on keeping his clubhouse light. You don't get down, everything is all right, you don't worry about it," Skidmore said. "Whatever the opposite of that is, that's what the clubhouse was like in 1969."

Along with other youngsters, the 23-year-old Skidmore was sent to Arizona for winter ball before the 1969 season ended. He had experienced the fall firsthand, but he was not there for the team's ultimate collapse.

"I didn't get the privilege of seeing the last day of the year when all the air went out of the Cubs," Skidmore said. "I saw most of it going out in September, but not all of it."

It was back to the drawing board. Skidmore had been in Chicago for three weeks and didn't sniff the field. With Ernie Banks supposedly entering his final season, Skidmore felt confident he could make the Cubs Opening Day roster in 1970. He had a solid spring training, but he was the last man cut from the roster. Chicago decided to stick with veteran left-handed hitter Al Spangler instead. Skidmore was told to go get work in Triple-A and he'd be up soon.

"Soon" became September, when once again Skidmore was a September call-up, not exactly the type of player Durocher was likely to slot into his lineup on any given day.

"I don't want to say Leo had something against the young guys, but you had to do something pretty special to prove yourself to even get in there," Skidmore recalled. This is the sort of sentiment indicative of the mentality necessary to remain vigilant in the face of countless setbacks and denials; even if there appeared to be a bias keeping him off the field, Skidmore saw it as the player's responsibility to get himself into the game.

Expecting to get some playing time, to get a taste of first base at Wrigley Field, Skidmore watched as Banks continued to play almost every inning of every game. The same names—Banks, Beckert, Kessinger, Santo, Billy Williams, Hundley—were in the lineup day after day despite the 1970 Cubs having no shot at the pennant.

September 17 came, and for the first time in Skidmore's professional career, everything lined up perfectly. It was an overcast day on the North Side of Chicago.[5] The Cubs and Cardinals, bitter rivals, were set for a late-season clash. A little rainy weather couldn't keep the Cubs faithful away.

"The whole park was packed on a Wednesday afternoon," Skidmore said. "Cubs fans are really something special."

By chance, Skidmore's high school baseball coach Clete Hinton, by this time a junior college coach in Chicago, was at Wrigley Field that day.[6] He and Skidmore chatted near the field before the game began, reminiscing on the state title they had won eight years earlier. Hinton went back to his seat and settled in for the rivalry game.

St. Louis struck first, as Jerry Reuss and Lou Brock slugged back-to-back singles to give the Cardinals the first two runs of the game. They poured it on in the third as Joe Torre, Jose Cardenal, Ed Crosby, and Brock all had RBI hits in the inning, pushing the advantage to 6–0. By the time the seventh inning rolled around, Chicago was down 8–1.

Ernie Banks led off the inning by flying out to center field. Randy Hundley followed with a groundout to shortstop. With two outs in the seventh inning, Durocher finally called Skidmore's number. He was sent to pinch-hit for the pitcher, Joe Decker.

"My knees were knocking together so much, I could hardly walk," Skidmore said.

He walked over to the bat rack, and a slow but quiet panic set in. He couldn't find his bat. Clubhouse attendants would generally put three to four of each player's bats in the rack. Skidmore couldn't find a single one of his. After what lasted ten seconds and felt like two minutes, trying to act like he knew what he was doing, Skidmore grabbed backup catcher J. C. Martin's bat.

"That's the part I remember the most: I couldn't find my stinking bat," Skidmore said. "I thought that was the beginning. Little did I know, that was the end."

Skidmore strolled to the plate for his first career at bat. Neither of his parents were in attendance. His dad was back at the shoe store working. The elder Roe never took a lunch break. He would take a sandwich to work and walk back and forth between the back room and the front room where customers were. In the back room, he had a radio always tuned to the Cubs game.

He walked to the back room while eating his sandwich and heard his son's name called. By chance, he heard that Roe was coming up to pinch-hit. Customers in the front room would have to wait. He listened as his son's every move was described over the radio.

"It's like it's in slow motion," Skidmore said. "I can still see in my mind's eye, walking up there. I couldn't get my arms to move."

That explains why he hit Jerry Reuss's first pitch about 100 feet foul down the right-field line. Reuss delivered again—a ball. Then he left a hanging breaking ball over the plate.

"At least it wasn't a cheap hit," Skidmore said. "I have that to hang on to."

He drove the ball to his pull field. For a second, it seemed like the at bat might end in heartbreak.

"I still remember Joe Torre jumping and he almost caught it," Skidmore recalled. "It went just over the top of his glove."

It landed safely in the left-field grass then was scooped up by Lou Brock and thrown back to the infield. Almost caught by Torre, fielded by Brock. Skidmore, who had just laced his first big-league hit, was star-struck.

"Two years before that, I had baseball cards of all these guys, looking at their face on a baseball card and now I'm out there watching them pick up the ball I hit and throw it in," Skidmore said, still in disbelief.

As the announcement of Skidmore's first hit came over the radio waves, the slugger's father went nuts. He jumped up and down with excitement and threw shoes all around the store.

"He probably celebrated more than I did," Skidmore said.

His mother heard his hit on the car radio as well.

"I guess God knew the day I was going to get a hit, so he positioned my mom, dad, and high school coach and put them in position so they could hear it or see it," Skidmore said.

It was a divine defensive shift, indeed.

Skidmore's time on the base paths didn't last long. Kessinger, the next batter, grounded to second base, forcing Skidmore out. He trotted back to the dugout and his day was done. Jim Dunegan, the man he signed autographs with in Tacoma when they both found out they'd made the big leagues in 1969, was replacing him in the lineup as the Cubs' new pitcher.

Skidmore went the rest of the 1970 season without playing in another big-league game. Ernie Banks decided to come back for the 1971 season. Skidmore was traded across town to the White Sox that winter. Outfielder Jose Ortiz came to the Cubs in the deal. After a solid spring training where he could have won the White Sox first-base job, more bad news came.

"About five or six days before the end of the spring, I picked up the newspaper before I went to the park for the last week of spring training," Skidmore recalled. "The headline read, 'White Sox get Richie Allen in a trade.' I could see the writing on the wall."

As soon as he got to the park, he was asked to the manager's office. He was being sent back to Triple-A. In 1971, Skidmore hit .299 with 20 home runs and 77 RBIs. Again, it wasn't good enough to get him a big-league call-up. Right as he was hitting his stride in 1972, he was traded once again, this time to the Cincinnati Reds.

At Triple-A Indianapolis, he was teammates with George Foster, Ken Griffey Sr., Ray Knight, and Joaquin Andujar, among others. He put up similar or better numbers than some of his teammates who went on to be stars. Six of them went on to be a part of the Big Red Machine a few years later. [7]

"I kept going along for several years, but I never could get in the right place at the right time," Skidmore said. "That's not sour grapes. That's just the way the business is."

Standing in front of him in Cincinnati was future Hall of Fame first baseman Tony Perez.

Skidmore was traded to the Cardinals before the 1974 season. Scooping him up, and saving his father from heartbreak, the Astros purchased Skidmore's contract before the 1974 season began. After the 1974 season, he was traded once again, this time to the Red Sox organization. He played just 12 games in Triple-A Pawtucket in 1975 before retiring.

"If I had to do it all over again, I'd probably stay in the game as a coach or manager, because that feeling has never left me," Skidmore said.

He, instead, returned home to a more steady job to take care of his growing family. He's still been involved in baseball over the years, serving as an area scout for the Phillies and Orioles for nearly a decade. Had there been as many teams in 1970 as there are now, Skidmore has no doubt he would have stuck with a club.

"Surely, I would have gotten a job for a few years," Skidmore theorized. "I guess you never know. I can't help but think about it over the years, but if it had happened now, I would have gotten to play for who knows how long."

Skidmore has a case. He recorded 1,157 minor-league hits, 390 of them extra-base hits to go along with 714 RBIs. All anyone ever wants to talk about with him, though, is his *one* hit: the one that counts.

"When I think back on all I did in the minor leagues, I wonder, 'Why didn't I get another shot?'" Skidmore questioned. "That was back then. Now, thinking back on it, it's wonderful."

While he's now more at peace with the way his career played out in his twilight years, Skidmore can't help but feel that childhood rush come back to him every new baseball season, as he longs for those halcyon days.

"I'm 72 years old and I swear every year in February, I go through a period of withdrawal for two weeks," Skidmore said. "That's pretty weird, because I haven't played for 40 years. . . . It just gets in your blood."

When you grow up in Decatur, Illinois, you either root for the Cubs or the Cardinals, and the Skidmores bled Cubby Blue. They still do. Roe himself had notched a base hit against them at Wrigley Field one overcast day in September.

"I played for several different organizations, but in the morning when I'd get up, I'd always get the paper and look at the box score to see if the Cubs won or not," Skidmore said.

He was used to rooting for a losing team, but lately, his favorite baseball team, the one he played for one September afternoon, has been winning. His youngest daughter, an oncologist in Tucson, Arizona, was due to have a baby in October 2016. That baby is now among the most spoiled Cubs fans to ever live.

Soon after his birth, the Cubs squared off with the Indians in Game Seven of the 2016 World Series. Skidmore and his family watched the decisive game from his daughter's house in Arizona.

"We were all jumping around, going nuts when they won," Skidmore said. "It got a little tense there at the end." The Cubs blew a late lead, something he'd seen them do countless times, some even from the Chicago dugout. This time, however, the story ended differently. In the final play of a game for the ages, Bryant threw to Rizzo and the Cubs were world champs.

The Cubs Skidmore had grown up rooting for, and then playing for, were no longer cursed. His celebration wasn't over. He had a phone call to make.

"My dad was back in Decatur," Skidmore said. "We talked on the phone. I called him and he was absolutely thrilled."

At 100 years old, the elder Skidmore had held on for a century in order to see his favorite team win the World Series. But the feeling paled in comparison to the afternoon when his own son suited up for the Cubs and slapped a base hit in his only career at bat. That ball, which sat safely on the Wrigley Field grass for a few precious seconds, still sits on Skidmore's mantel, yellowing with age.

"It just says, 'First big-league hit,'" Skidmore said with a smile.

"I didn't have the heart to write 'Last big-league hit' on it too."

3

LARRY YOUNT

September 15, 1971

Walking down Ventura Boulevard, a young Larry Yount's eyes darted around, catching the surrounding pageantry. Baseball was in the air. It was Opening Day. In the late 1950s, Little League still meant something and the league's opening day was something worth throwing a parade over. Parades and other baseball-related events introduced Yount to the game. It was through the excitement such events generated that his love for baseball was born.

He listened to Dodgers games on the radio. They were the new team in town, fresh off fulfilling their own manifest destiny, and a young broadcaster named Vin Scully was in the first of his seven decades as the beloved voice of the franchise.

"Listening to the Dodgers on the radio with Vin Scully broadcasting, that was a big deal," Yount said.

His early baseball memories continued to foster a love for the game. Yount's grandfather, an avid Cincinnati Reds fan, took him to a double-header at Crosley Field in his childhood.

"We got there in time for batting practice," Yount said. "We were along the rail and they were taking batting practice. Johnny Edwards broke his bat and waved me onto the field to come get it." It was the first time someone would call him onto a major-league field.

That bat became one of Yount's most prized possessions. As the years went by, he turned passion into promise as he played his way onto an elite

Pony League team. His team reached the Pony League World Series in 1963 when he was 13 years old.

"Some way, somehow, I figured out how to throw a breaking ball," Yount said. "I was really good at it. I was the smallest guy on the team

Larry Yount in uniform for Taft High School in 1968 before getting picked in the fifth round of the June draft. *Courtesy of Larry Yount*

and a relief pitcher. All I did was come in and throw curveballs." Most boys who went through Little League remember the first kid who figured out how to throw junk. For a time, he became virtually unhittable.

His younger brother, Robin, eight years old at the time, was the team's batboy.

Larry and Robin were raised by intellectual, unathletic parents, Marion and Phil. It was hardly the household you'd expect two future professional ballplayers to come from. Phil was literally a rocket scientist. The move to California was precipitated by a job he took with Rocketdyne where he was the head of quality control, in charge of building rocket engines.

"It's not typical for two baseball players to come out of that situation," Larry Yount said.

Throwing strikes isn't rocket science, but for some pitchers, throwing strikes with breaking balls is just as hard. That was never the case for Yount, which helped to separate him from many of his contemporaries. With the help of his right arm, his Pony League team finished second in the country that season, losing in the championship. Through a tournament blind draw, he was selected to throw out the first pitch at a Dodgers game. He wouldn't be throwing out the first pitch of just any Dodgers game. The game he got to throw the first pitch at? Game Five of the 1963 World Series.

This set of cosmic events, that random selection and its aftermath, served as cruel foreshadowing for how his professional career would play out. Yount would not get to throw out that pitch, because the series never reached a fifth game.

"I can remember distinctly, sitting in my car, listening to the fourth game of the World Series when the Dodgers won four straight," Yount said. "I remember how crushed I was that I wasn't going to get to do something pretty unbelievable."

The Dodgers swept the Yankees in the '63 fall classic, and Yount was despondent. Not getting to throw out that first pitch still stands out as his most distinct baseball memory. Luckily for Yount, someone with the Dodgers was looking out for him.

"The Dodgers, to their credit, had somebody there who had enough sense to understand what a crushing blow that was to a 13-year-old boy who thought he was going to throw out the ball," Yount said, "so, they invited me to throw out the Opening Day ball in 1964." Yount would later see that this concern for fairness did not extend to professional ballplayers, but for now it appeared that the game he loved did, indeed, love him back.

Yount ended up throwing out the first pitch of the 1964 season as the Dodgers were celebrated as the defending world champions. He threw the ball to Johnny Roseboro, a moment he said he will never forget. Afterward, he sat in the dugout with Jeff Torborg and chatted with him about the game they shared a passion for. The likes of Sandy Koufax and Don Drysdale passed through the dugout as their conversation went on.

It was a moment that would motivate the teenager to pursue his dream. For Yount, that dream was pitching in the major leagues. On a perfect April afternoon in LA, his desire was reaffirmed. Yount shed the label of a small, specialty relief pitcher by his junior year of high school. He shot up and developed a deeper arsenal of pitches. With a bigger frame, he was throwing harder, adding a fastball to his already polished off-speed attack.

Pitching for Taft High School in Woodland Hills, California, Yount caught the eyes of more than a few scouts. When he was taken by the Houston Astros in the fifth round of the 1968 MLB draft, he was too young and cocky to recognize the moment's importance.[1]

"I didn't think anything about it. I thought it made sense. I thought I was pretty good, I guess," Yount said. "When I got drafted, I actually went out of high school to Triple-A, which was not typical even back then. I didn't know any better."

Yount, just 18 years old when the Astros selected him, was put on the fast track. He spent his first several spring trainings in big-league camp. Ignorance was bliss as Yount worked his way through the Houston system. The naïveté of his youth served him well.

"It certainly was an asset," Yount said. "If you never know the rest of them are chasing you, you don't know who might be gaining on you."

In his first spring training appearance, Yount looked down at the signs from his catcher as he prepared to throw his first professional pitch. Staring back at him was Johnny Edwards, the former Reds catcher who had waved him onto the field when he was a child. Yount recalls a brief conversation between the two before the game.

"Johnny, I was a little kid, remember when you gave me that bat?" Yount asked.

"Get out of here, kid," Edwards said, or something along those lines as Yount remembered. Welcome to the big leagues.

By his second year in professional baseball, it was clear he had the capability to pitch in the major leagues on a regular basis. After getting the growing pains out of the way, spread between Single-A and Triple-A in 1968, Yount broke out in 1969. The Astros had pumped the brakes on him, which helped his development. He went a combined 11–6 with a 2.27 ERA split between winter rookie ball and Single-A in 1969, pitching a few levels below where he had begun his professional career.

The following season, he moved up to Double-A. With the Columbus Astros, he went 12–8 with a 2.84 ERA in 26 starts and hurled 11 complete games. It was the next step toward the big leagues as Yount started toward a more traditional route to the majors. By then, he was moving up one level of competition at a time.

He started 1971 in Triple-A Oklahoma City. He went 5–8 with a 4.86 ERA, a step below what he had done at the Double-A level. This time, though, he was going against harder competition. During the summer of 1973, Yount's younger brother, Robin, now a budding high school star, spent time with Larry and his Denver Bears teammates.

"He would come out for a week or two where we were taking batting practice," Yount said. "That helped him realize he could play with the people on the field."

When he arrived home from hitting against Triple-A pitchers as a teenager, Robin reportedly got back to baseball practice as excited as ever. He told his high school coach, "I hit guys in Triple-A. They tried to get me out and I still hit them. . . . I think I'm going to have a pretty good year."

One could loosely characterize his next two decades as "pretty good."

Since he was busy forging his professional baseball career, Larry did not get to see Robin's ascent in the sport. However, gestures like his invitation to Robin to join the team during the summer showed how invested Larry was in his younger brother's future. He played a big role in his development as Robin, too, rose through the ranks young, eventually making his major-league debut at 18.

"I don't think we knew he was going to be this great baseball player until really late in high school," Larry said. "I was gone playing professional baseball at that point. I don't think I ever saw him play in a high school game."

When Oklahoma City's season ended in 1971, Yount was called up to the Astros. Before he could join Houston, he was required to attend an army reserve meeting.

Spurred on by the Vietnam War, Yount and many others were in the army reserve at the time, and as part of his duties, he had a mandatory meeting, lasting several days. It just happened to fall in the time when his Oklahoma City season ended and he got the call from Houston.

Without a mitt or a ball, Yount was unable to throw and keep his arm loose during the several days he was away. Throughout his career, any rustiness he felt in his arm was caused by underuse, not overuse. Eventually, Yount had fulfilled his obligation and was, at last, set to join the Astros.

"Somehow, I ended up in Atlanta," Yount said. "I'm still not sure how I got there."

He didn't get there. Maybe Yount has tried to block it out or the baseball memories have melted together over the years, but the Astros weren't playing in Atlanta. Yes, they were playing the Braves, but the series was at the Astrodome in Houston.

On September 15, 1971, neither the Astros nor Braves were in contention for a playoff spot. There were only 6,500 fans on hand for the game. They all were buzzing when, in the top of the fifth inning, Hank Aaron clubbed career home run number 636. It gave him 1,954 career RBIs, tying him with Ty Cobb for third on the all-time list.[2]

Yount doesn't have a strong recollection of this or much else that went on during the game. He had a laser focus out in the bullpen, hoping his first chance to pitch in a big-league game would come.

"I didn't think very much," Yount said. "I was paying attention to what I was doing, so I really didn't see what was going on. Having said that, I knew my arm was getting pretty sore."

With his team trailing 4–1 late, Yount was told he would come in to pitch in the top of the ninth inning. He started to warm up. Immediately, he knew something was wrong. He willed his arm to get better with each subsequent warm-up pitch, but the pain wouldn't go away.

"I hoped it would feel better when I got to the mound," Yount said. "There was a lot of hope it would happen or I wouldn't have gone in."

Someone with his level of discomfort would never be thrust into a game in the modern day. In 1971, though, a 21-year-old trying to prove himself wasn't going to let anything stand between him and pitching in his first big-league game. He was sure the soreness would go away once the adrenaline started coursing through his veins.

Joe Morgan grounded out to end the home half of the eighth inning. Then, the public address announcer went over the intercom to announce that Larry Yount would be entering the game for the Astros. There it was: Yount was officially in the major-league record books. Yount trotted out to the mound, trying to work the rust out of his arm, rust he is convinced was caused by his weeklong army reserve layoff.

"It was getting progressively worse, so I knew that it wasn't going to just be a miracle and go away at that point," Yount said. "I was just hoping, because I wanted to go in. . . . I wanted to be in that game more than anything in the world."

Due up for the Braves in the ninth were Felix Millan, Ralph Garr, and Hank Aaron. That season, Millan was an all-star. Garr batted .343 in 1971. Aaron was in the midst of giving the Sultan of Swat a run for his money. Yount had his work cut out for him.

"That would have been an interesting way to start a career," Yount joked.

However, as he got down to his last few warm-up pitches, Yount realized he would be putting his young arm in harm's way if he tried to pitch. He had a decade or more ahead of him. It was the smart move to make sure he escaped further injury by avoiding putting his arm under the physical pressure required to throw in a major-league game. He made one of the hardest decisions a professional athlete has ever been asked to make. At the time, it was a straightforward one.

"After throwing a couple warm-ups, I thought, 'If I keep this up and really try to do what I need to do to get somebody out, I could hurt myself,'" Yount recalled. "At 21 years old, generally, you don't make rational decisions, but I had enough sense not to take the chance."

Yount pulled himself from the game. He wasn't physically capable of pitching effectively. Reliever Jim Ray was called in to replace him.

"It's not an easy thing to do when you're getting your opportunity, but I did and I came out of the game without throwing any pitches," Yount said.

Yount didn't throw a single pitch, but he was credited with a major-league appearance. MLB rules state the announced pitcher must start the inning, unless they are removed due to injury. At just 21 years old and pitching better than he ever had to that point in his career, there was no reason for Yount to take a risk on his future by pitching on September 15, 1971.

Ray pitched a scoreless ninth, the Astros scratched across a run in their last time up and lost 4–2. Yount's sore elbow kept him out of the rest of the 1971 season with the belief he had a very good chance of making the Opening Day roster in 1972. He did have a reasonable beat on a spot in the starting rotation.

After the 1971 season, Yount pitched effectively in the instructional league, his elbow soreness gone within two weeks of his lone MLB "appearance" to that point. He came into spring training the following season and continued to impress. He was competing with two other pitchers, Scipio Spinks and Tom Griffin, for a spot in the Astros' starting rotation. Spinks and Griffin were out of options; Yount was not.

"I made one bad pitch all spring," Yount recalled to *Astros Magazine* in 1989. "It was a three-run homer to Willie Davis and it was right when they had to make the decision."

The Davis homer didn't help, but cutting Yount from the big-league roster was a business decision. Yount was player no. 26, the final player sent down before the 25-man roster was etched in stone. He was sent back to Oklahoma City. There, he started 3–0, looking as if he'd soon join the Astros rotation for good. Before he had the chance, the wheels fell off.

"I started having some things not go well and I started thinking about, 'Why am I not throwing strikes? I've thrown strikes my whole life,'" Yount remembered pondering. "I managed to figure out, mentally, how to screw up a pretty good thing."

Accuracy with his breaking ball had been Yount's calling card since he was in Pony League. Now, it was accuracy that was threatening to derail his promising professional career. Yount pitched in Triple-A in each of his next two seasons, going a combined 8–26 with ERAs of 5.15 and 6.79, respectively.

Sensing his best years were behind him, the Astros traded Yount to the Brewers, the franchise that had just selected his brother, Robin, third overall in the 1973 MLB draft when he was just 17 years old. Larry said the two never crossed paths in spring training.[3] Cuts had already been made by the time Larry arrived. Robin was now 18 and it was his first spring training. He made the big-league club, playing in 107 games his rookie year. Larry didn't play at all in 1974.

"I was hoping somehow, somebody would tell me something to figure out how to throw strikes," Yount said. "That didn't happen. I was always struggling to figure that out. . . . I just couldn't throw strikes anymore. Once that happens, it's not easy to correct."

Yount even went back to Taft High School to talk to his former coach, Ray O'Connor, he told the *Los Angeles Times* in 1994. His coach recalled him as a somewhat arrogant pitcher during his high school days. When he watched him late in his professional career, he saw a pitcher with the opposite demeanor. He was lost.

The 1975 season was Larry's final trip around the bases. He had sought out psychological advice, anything that would help him regain his mental edge. Some advice helped; other advice didn't. At 25 years old, his life was really just beginning. His professional baseball career was just ending. He went 0–4 with a 5.32 ERA in Single-A and 8–12 with a 4.74 ERA in Double-A in 1975. After the season, he called it quits.

Yount never got back to the big leagues. Moonlight Graham's career is one someone with Yount's experience might envy. At least Graham was standing on the field when pitches were thrown. Yount got as close as you can possibly get to reaching the pinnacle of your profession— pitching in a major-league game—without actually getting there. He is quick to point out that his injury and decision to remove himself from the game is not what kept him from having a successful big-league career.

"I don't think about that moment much, because I had plenty of opportunity afterward," Yount said. "I certainly don't look at that as 'would I have done it differently?' I wouldn't have, because after the fact, I was very good and had every opportunity." Though he said he seldom thinks about it, this sort of clarity hardly comes without some significant time spent reflecting.

Yount is still the only pitcher in major-league history to be credited with an appearance without facing one batter in his career. He is a statistical anomaly, a tragic footnote on the history of the game. Just 25 years old, Yount, without the game he grew up on, now had the rest of his life to look forward to.

"I didn't want to try and raise a family in Los Angeles," Yount said. "So, we moved to Arizona and I got a real estate license and went to work."

Yount had gotten a real estate license during his season in the instructional league following his one appearance in 1971. He said he mostly got the license to pass the time. It ended up changing his postbaseball life. After his first few years in Arizona, he decided to learn the business by going out on his own. He learned every part of the business, building an industrial building, shopping center, and office while overseeing building, leasing, financing, and managing. Over his 40 years in the business, he built a multimillion-dollar company, LKY Advisors, LLC. After a lifetime of work, Larry Yount was a success. It wasn't the success he'd once pictured for himself, but it was a success all his own.

He continued to be involved in baseball through his brother, Robin, who quickly budded into one of the sport's biggest stars while playing for the Brewers.

"I represented my brother in his contract negotiations, so I was always interacting with Bud [Selig]," Yount said. "Any contract negotiations he had, I was in the middle of them."

Yount befriended then Brewers owner and future MLB commissioner Bud Selig, and the two are still friends to this day. While Yount wasn't ultimately the one to deliver a major-league franchise to Phoenix, he did mention the potential expansion location to Selig on several occasions. About a decade after he and several others had made a push in the late 1980s to get an expansion team to Phoenix, the area landed the Diamondbacks in 1998 under the leadership of Jerry Colangelo.[4]

In the lead-up to the Diamondbacks, Yount worked as the president of the Triple-A Phoenix Thunderbirds in the 1990s under team owner Martin Stone, a catalyst for the move of both the NFL's Cardinals and the MLB's Diamondbacks to the area.[5]

Yount still throws the ball around from time to time. As he built his real estate business, he saw his children mature, improving upon baseball skills their dad had learned around their age as well.

"It's certainly fun to throw baseballs to your kids," Yount said. "There's nothing more fun than that."

Even as his kids grew up, he kept trying to figure out what had gone wrong with him mentally during his playing days. As he played baseball with his kids in a more relaxed environment, some answers started coming to him. Of course, by then, too much time had passed.

"I'll always wonder why I couldn't figure out how to get back to where I was," Yount said. "I was lucky enough to throw batting practice afterward to my two boys and slowly, but surely, I began to figure out some of the things I couldn't figure out, but at that point in time, I was too old." That sort of clarity paired with productive athletic years is a privilege afforded to a fortunate few.

As Austin and Cody Yount grew up, it was apparent they had the same raw potential their dad did. They would not be like their dad in one respect, and it was through his own experience Larry made sure this was the case.

"The thing Rob and I did not do is get a college education and the thing I was going to be sure of was my kids all did," Yount said. "At some point in time, you realize no matter how great you are, your career is over and you have to do something else. Having an education is invaluable."

Austin went to Stanford and was selected in the 12th round of the 2008 MLB draft by the Los Angeles Dodgers, the team his dad had thrown out the first pitch for on Opening Day 44 years prior. He played parts of four seasons in the minor leagues, reaching as far as the High-A Winston-Salem Dash.[6] Cody was picked in the 37th round of the 2013 MLB draft by the Chicago White Sox. After two seasons in rookie ball, he was out of Organized Baseball, not afforded the chance to skip the low levels of the minor leagues like his dad and uncle were.[7]

Robin Yount played 20 years in the big leagues, joining the 3,000-hit club and becoming one of the greatest players in Brewers history. He was inducted into the National Baseball Hall of Fame in 1999. Baseball fans know Robin Yount's name. Very few know Larry's. Success in baseball, though, isn't the only measure of success in life. Larry has lived nearly 50 years without playing baseball competitively and, had he gotten a chance in the majors, he doesn't think the life he's grown to love would even resemble what it is today.

"If I had been in the big leagues for any length of time, my whole life would be different," Yount said. "I probably wouldn't be married to the same person, I wouldn't have my kids, I wouldn't be in the real estate business the way I was. That probably would have been a huge, huge difference in my life, that path change."

He added, "My life couldn't have been any better. I overachieved so much. All of that was just a moment in time."

A moment in time: something Yount got to experience on a major-league mound for a few fleeting seconds, never to return to pitch in another big-league game. To get that close and not throw a pitch, it's hard not to wonder "what if." Nearly half a century removed from his one moment in the sun, Yount is ecstatic with the way his life has played out. He talks about the things he's accomplished, his mark on the sport, and the kids he's raised to love the game, with the excitement of a Little Leaguer, eyes darting side to side, marching in an opening day parade down Ventura Boulevard.

4

GARY MARTZ

July 8, 1975

It started when Kansas City Athletics owner Charles Finley decided he was fed up with the city. The legendary owner no longer wanted to call KC home and, in 1967, made up his mind that he would relocate the franchise. An option he seriously considered was Seattle, the country's third-largest city in the West. However, the stadium already in place, Sick's Stadium, had a name very descriptive of its condition.

In the end, Finley decided to move the franchise to Oakland, where it still is more than 50 years later. Feeling miffed by the Athletics' departure, though, Missouri senator Stuart Symington threatened to bring legislation forward that would challenge Major League Baseball's reserve clause if KC didn't get another team. His threat was so effective, it forces one to wonder why others didn't employ the reserve clause before its abolishment in 1975. Either way, Kansas City fans are grateful for Senator Symington's efforts: feeling the pressure, Major League Baseball added a team to Kansas City that would begin play in 1969. The new franchise would be named the "Royals."[1]

Naturally, the league couldn't have an odd number of teams, so they had to add another to balance out the addition of the Royals. These two franchises initially were set to open play in 1971, but more pressure from Symington forced the league to add the teams for the 1969 season. As it would prove, this early start date would doom the second franchise.

Seattle had had a Pacific Coast League franchise since the 1938 season. The Pacific Coast League is the same league that produced players like Ted Williams and Joe DiMaggio and sold them to major-league franchises. Local brewer Emil Sick, bought the Pacific Northwest League's Seattle Braves and instantly renamed them the "Rainiers" after both his brewery and the famous Washington mountain.[2]

For 30 years, Sick wanted to prove his city was capable of housing a major-league baseball team. Despite that desire, the short amount of time to get a major-league ballclub together would prove to be a challenge. Seattle, indeed, was awarded the American League's second new franchise, which would be named the "Pilots." In the team's first draft in 1969, they took Gorman Thomas with the 21st overall pick, making him the first draft selection in Seattle Pilots history.[3] With their fourth pick (in the fifth round), they selected a right-handed power hitter named Gary Martz.

Martz grew up in Spokane, just 280 miles east of Seattle. By his sophomore year at West Valley High School, he was dominating opposing pitching, earning the attention of several big-league ballclubs. He tried to emulate Mickey Mantle, his idol. The Mick was everything he wanted to be in a ballplayer: "He's one of those guys who would just give you 100 percent and never complain about anything. He just went out there and busted his butt," Martz said.

The young slugger busted his own butt in high school, and it paid off. When he was drafted by the Pilots in the fifth round, he couldn't wait to sign on the dotted line.

"I was just elated. I didn't come down until after I actually signed the contract," Martz said. "In hindsight, that's one of the bigger mistakes I ever made."

Martz's high school and American Legion coaches told him signing a professional contract was a mistake, but he wasn't having any of it. Even though he had a baseball scholarship to Washington State University and a football scholarship to the University of Idaho to play quarterback, his dream was clear.

"Lifetime-wise, I would have been much better off if I'd gone to college, but there's no way I was going to do that," Martz said. "My mind was set that if I ever had the chance, I was playing pro ball as soon as I could." The thinking may seem shortsighted, but through the accounts from cup of coffee guys like Larry Yount, one can see the merit in seizing opportunity the moment it presents itself. You never know when (or if) the opportunity will come around again.

In the 1960s, signing out of high school was the norm. Unlike modern baseball, college ball wasn't seen as a prerequisite to the major leagues for most.

"There weren't all that many kids being signed out of college," Martz recalled. "If you had a chance to sign out of high school, that was by far your best chance."

The instruction Martz was expecting when he arrived in Billings, Montana, for rookie league in 1969 was simply nonexistent. Even in future years in the minor leagues, Martz didn't have many instructors helping him along.

"I played nine years in the minor leagues and we never had more than a manager," Martz said. "There wasn't a pitching coach and there wasn't a hitting coach."

It hurt his performance as he hit just .264 with six home runs and 40 RBIs in 66 games in Billings. The Arizona Fall League was even worse. In 23 games, he hit .164 with no home runs and four RBIs.[4] As he continued through the minor leagues, the lack of instruction and personal struggles sent him inside of his own head.

"Especially for a person like me, who rationalizes everything and plays mind games, it was tough," Martz said. "It would've been nice to have somebody who would sit down and just say, 'To heck with all that, just work on this, this, and this and forget about everything else.'"

Spring training and the instructional league were essentially Martz's only opportunities to get one-on-one time with skilled instructors. Most other training resources went toward the major-league club, a decision that seems interesting given the goal is to develop players to reach the major leagues, not merely stay there.

Martz's dreams of playing in Seattle were dashed when the team became the first and only franchise in MLB history to go bankrupt. Just days before the 1970 season began, they picked up and moved to Milwaukee, where they changed their name to the Brewers.[5] The rush to get Seattle a team ahead of when the city and ownership were ready led, in part, to their untimely departure. Players in the lower levels of the minor leagues were not aware just how dire the situation was.

"It really surprised the heck out of me," Martz remembered. "It was really disappointing. I was looking forward to playing in Seattle one day and Milwaukee was a different planet as far as I was concerned. . . . It would have been different if it turned out to be Boston or New York, but Milwaukee? Not to say anything bad about Milwaukee—they make great beer."

The Pilots' short stay in Seattle turned them into a blip on the radar of baseball history. In fact, when Martz brings it up now, it confuses people.

"I mention to people I signed with the Seattle Pilots and they say, 'Huh? What the hell is that?'"

Martz continued, "In Spokane, I'd tell people the last 10 to 20 years about my career and they didn't even know Seattle had a team before the Mariners."

His early days in baseball, at least as far as his initial franchise is concerned, were lost in the annals of history.

For the next three seasons, now with the goal of reaching Milwaukee, Martz lived in towns with which career minor leaguers are all familiar. His first stop was A-ball in Clinton, Iowa, in his first full season, 1970. Then, 1971 saw him go to Newark, New York, as a member of the Low-A Co-Pilots. After once being a Pilot, Martz had become a Co-Pilot. The life of a minor-league journeyman is often fraught with such irony. Finally, in 1972 and still in A-ball, he got to call the metropolis of Danville, Illinois, home.

With the help of a Brewers connection in Glendale, Arizona, he joined an army reserve unit, a sure way to avoid fighting a brutal war in Vietnam.

"This was early in the Vietnam War era when they had the draft," Martz said. "Everybody and their dog was trying to get in a reserve unit so they wouldn't get drafted and have to go to Vietnam."

Between 1970 and 1972, he hit no higher than .272 and hit no more than 12 home runs as a right-handed power hitter. However, in 1973, he was given a chance in Double-A to show he was more than an organizational player. He didn't disappoint.

Martz hit 34 home runs and drove in 154 over the next two seasons in Shreveport while batting .291 in 1973 and .293 in 1974. It was clearly the breakout his career needed, but still in Double-A, he didn't feel his dream was anywhere close to being realized.

"I never signed a big-league contract, so I never went to big-league spring training or got called up in September," Martz said. "The big leagues, at that point, really seemed a long way away."

Then, as it must for a fringe player to eventually crack the big leagues, Martz caught a break. Ahead of the 1975 season, the 24-year-old was traded from the Brewers to the Kansas City Royals, the very team whose formation necessitated the creation of his initial franchise. In point of fact, his contract was actually sold to KC.[6] Instantly, Martz saw how important the move was for his career.

"Organization-wise, Kansas City was just light-years ahead of Milwaukee," Martz said.

On top of that, the Royals started Martz off in Triple-A, just one call from the big leagues. Only one level ahead of where he was with the Brewers, he noticed the travel and amenities were night and day compared to what he'd grown used to in the lower levels of the minor leagues.

In Shreveport, the Captains were on the far eastern edge of the Double-A Texas League. When they had to play El Paso, the trip turned into an all-day, all-night affair. By the time the team left Shreveport following a game and after grabbing a burger from McDonald's, it was midnight.

From there, they would drive 17 to 18 hours, which got them to the field at 5:00 or 6:00 p.m. The game started at 7:30. Needless to say, there was no stopping at the hotel; they went straight to the field.

In Triple-A, Martz's travel shifted from the ground to the air.

"It was unbelievable," Martz said. "Most of our road trips, we flew. Even in Double-A, at least with Milwaukee, everything was by bus. . . . Being able to fly in Triple-A was like I died and went to heaven."

The Royals even had a "Baseball Academy," which they used to train talented athletes. The franchise had a philosophy that it could draft raw athletes and turn them into elite baseball players. It was unique thinking at the time, but it didn't last long.

"It was a great concept, but they gave up on it after about six years, because they realized it takes a different breed of cat to play baseball," Martz said.

The best athletes in the world can't crack it in baseball if they don't have the mental fortitude to spend years in the minor leagues honing their craft. It's only after that apprenticeship that they can be ready for the spotlight of the major leagues. Patience and dedication are among the baseline requirements to become a successful major leaguer.

"I'm convinced it really takes a different mind-set to be a baseball player," Martz opined. "Being a great athlete definitely helps, but you have to be able to go to bed at night, wake up in the morning, and forget exactly how many times you struck out the night before. . . . That was always a bugaboo of mine. I had power, but boy, I liked to swing at everything."

Martz swung (and hit) his way through Triple-A pitching, slugging at the most impressive clip of his career. He was doing all of this in Omaha, one call from the big leagues. When star Kansas City outfielder Amos Otis's throat started hurting, it opened the door for Martz to get his shot.

Otis ended up needing a tonsillectomy and was placed on the 15-day disabled list. In a corresponding move, the Royals had to call an outfielder up from the minors.[7]

Omaha manager Billy Gardner called Martz into his office shortly after Otis was placed on the DL. He told Martz to pack his bags—he was going to Kansas City.

"That was about it," Martz remembered of his moment of validation. "I somehow got our old family station wagon to fly down the highway to get to our apartment after the game. . . . It was everything I'd ever hoped for. That was the highlight."

Before he got to Kansas City, Martz had to meet the team in Texas where they were playing the Rangers. With a two-week time limit and as a reserve, Martz knew he likely wouldn't get into a game, but he was happy to be along for the ride.

"I always wanted to be a big leaguer. So, I accomplished that. My greatest goal in life, I accomplished," Martz said. "That first week on the road in Texas, I made almost as much in meal money as my salary was in Omaha." His life was a whirlwind.

Texas wasn't as glamorous as Martz had hoped. He related Arlington Stadium to some Triple-A stadiums in which he had played. What he returned to in Kansas City, however, was as big league as it came.

"When I got to Kansas City, that's when I saw what a real stadium was," Martz said. "That whole complex with Arrowhead Stadium, now that was state of the art."

Throughout that first series in Texas, one thing became clear to Martz: manager Jack McKeon was on his way out the door.

"When I was there, McKeon had totally lost the team," Martz remembered. "He alienated all the players and it was just a matter of time before he [was] fired. . . . He didn't even acknowledge I was there. I never did formally meet him. As far as I was concerned, he was a horse's ass and sadly, most players felt the same way. Even the stars didn't have any respect for him."

A manager in this sort of limbo, even with the Royals playing decent baseball, certainly had no incentive to play an unproven player like Martz. By the time July 8 rolled around, that hadn't changed.

Kansas City jumped out to a big lead against, of all teams, the Milwaukee Brewers at Royals Stadium. That night, more than 12,000 fans scattered the seats to see a Royals team that entered eight games over .500. Kansas City struck for five in the first and three in the fourth.

It was 8–1 in the eighth inning, and Martz's short stint with the major-league club was half over.[8] Hitting his reserve outfielder, even in a lopsided game, seemed like the last thing on McKeon's mind, though. That's when power-hitting first baseman John Mayberry stepped in and helped alter Martz's career. Mayberry walked up to his manager before the Royals batted in the eighth inning.

"Hey, why don't you let the kid hit for me?" Martz remembered Mayberry appealing to McKeon.

The skipper, having no real reason to care one way or the other, obliged, and Martz was due to bat third in the inning behind George Brett and Hal McRae, two players who would unbelievably still be on the team a decade later when they won their first World Series title.

"I thought that was awfully nice of Mayberry to do that," Martz said. "Then I thought about it some more. Mayberry didn't like lefty slider pitchers [pitcher Rick Austin was a lefty slider pitcher], so it was kind of self-serving suggesting I pinch-hit for him, because he didn't want to see another slider."

Martz chuckled as he recalled those gears turning in his head. He didn't care if the move was self-serving or not. It was a move that helped him get into a game he otherwise wouldn't have. The game, ultimately, which would prove to be his only one.

"Oh, I'm positive it wasn't McKeon's idea," Martz said. "I don't even think he knew I was sitting on the bench, to be honest with you."

Even if Mayberry had been merely avoiding pesky sliders by abdicating his AB to Martz, there still are other substitutes whom he could have suggested to his manager. Perhaps a common thread connecting one-game players is that they all, at one point or another, did something unforeseeably correct, like currying favor with John Mayberry, or maintaining a relationship with a particular scout, as was the case with Roe

Skidmore. For him, like many others, this singular validating moment came as the result of a collection of fortuitous events and decisions.

Regardless of the circumstances, Martz went from warming the bench to stepping into the batter's box in a matter of minutes.

"All of a sudden, I'm standing at home plate going, 'Holy shit, I'm actually going to bat,'" Martz recalled, knees shaking. "Needless to say, I swung at the first pitch. I think it could've been over my head and I would've swung at it."

It wasn't over his head. It was a slider in and Martz made good contact, but he hit the top half of the ball into the ground. It was a sharp one-hopper to Don Money, a sure double play. However, the pivot throw to first was airmailed, and Martz ended up with a fielder's choice and stood on second base as future Hall of Famer Harmon Killebrew stepped up to the plate.

Knowing his greatness, and admiring his attitude, Martz quickly befriended Killebrew when he arrived in Kansas City.

"I spent as much time as I could with Harmon," Martz said. "He was a neat guy, down to earth, and a sure Hall of Famer. I liked rubbing shoulders with him."

At the time, Killebrew was fifth on the all-time home-run list and was playing in his final big-league season.[9] With that in mind, on the night before what would be his debut, Martz devised a plan to get onto national television. The Royals were hosting the Brewers in the first game of their series on the nationally televised *Monday Night Baseball* program. Without playing, Martz didn't know how he would get on TV. Then he hatched his plan.

"I thought to myself, 'What's the best chance I have of getting on TV?'" Martz recalled. "Well, Harmon was DH-ing. I said, 'I'm going to sit next to Killebrew on the bench, because sooner or later, the cameras are going to look for baseball's next Hall of Famer.' . . . Sure as heck, my parents told me they saw me on TV sitting next to Harmon Killebrew."

On this night, though, the legend in the batter's box had the same luck as Martz. He topped a pitch sharply to third base and was thrown out. Martz was stranded on second when Rodney Scott followed suit by grounding out to third as well. Martz was sent to left field to play the top of the ninth and caught a Bill Sharp fly ball for the first out of the inning.

A Darrell Porter fly out to right field ended it as the Royals won the game, 9–1. Martz's big-league debut ended with a "W." Little did he know, there was a fan with a camera in the stands. Jack Rosensteel used his Polaroid to capture moments throughout the game, including Martz's one at bat, his short time in the field, and his name illuminated on the Royals' scoreboard above the Hall of Famer, Killebrew.

Eventually a letter, along with the photographs, found their way to Gary in the mail. In the letter, Pauline Rosensteel, the photographer's wife, wrote:

Dear Gary Martz,

My husband took these of you while you were in a Royal uniform and of the time you actually was [sic] a pinch hitter. We thought you and your wife would like them to maybe put in a scrap book. We hope you enjoy them, they're yours. Maybe we'll see you again in a Royal uniform.

Pauline and Jack Rosensteel

They wouldn't see him in a Royal uniform again, but those pictures are a way for Martz to remember his brush with the big leagues and the excitement with which it came.

After the game, Martz was invited to the Brewers' road poker game by Gorman Thomas, the Seattle Pilots' first and only first-round draft pick. The two had become close friends during their time in the Brewers' farm system.

"Gorman inviting me to that poker game, that was as exciting as getting into a big-league game," Martz said.

Thomas and some of the other Brewers were there. At one point, legendary play-by-play broadcaster Bob Uecker shuffled in to join the game.

"Gorman was the no. 1 draft choice, he had money, so I knew he would bluff every hand no matter what he had," Martz remembered as if he could still smell the cash. "I was used to taking his money. Then, Bob Uecker showed up and he was like Gorman, he didn't mind losing his money either."

His career had come strangely full circle. Though he did not get a hit in his only at bat, Martz played against the franchise that drafted him and, on the same night, played poker with his good friend, who happened to be that franchise's first-ever draft selection. If only every night in the big leagues could have been like that one.

After another week, Martz knew his time was up. Amos Otis's tonsils had been removed and he was completely healed. With Otis ready to return to the big-league roster, there was nowhere to put the power hitter from Spokane.

"Truthfully, I wouldn't have minded some complications that would've kept him on the disabled list a little longer," Martz said in jest.

Given the circumstances of his call-up, the trip back down to the minor leagues was no big deal. However, a couple of weeks later, a shake-up in the Royals' power structure altered the course of Martz's career.

Just 13 games after his debut and a week after he was sent back down to Triple-A, the Royals finally did what Martz had been figuring they'd do: they fired Jack McKeon. He was replaced with Whitey Herzog, who would lead the Royals to their first World Series title a decade later.

"I didn't think a change in manager would affect me that much," Martz remembered thinking at the time. "It turns out it did. I also understand it had to be done, but it didn't make it any easier for me."

Herzog favored working with core stars rather than rookies. That greatly diminished Martz's chance to earn another big-league shot, at least with the Royals.

"When September came around and I didn't get called up and big-league camp came around and I didn't get an invite, that's when I started wondering if this was just a flash in the pan and if that was going to be it," Martz said. He was coming to grips with a potentially grim reality.

He started pushing himself even harder to get back to the big leagues. Without a mental skills coach, which the majority of major-league teams now employ, he was lost at the plate and was in his own head.

"I tended to go into mental slumps where I'd just work too hard and it started dawning on me that's probably the one shot I'd ever have," Martz said, still sounding dejected.

His power numbers over the next two seasons held steady, but his other numbers dropped dramatically. He hit just .243 in 1976 and .217 in 1977. Clearly, his time with the Royals was finished. When Martz was just 26 years old and looking for direction, Kansas City did him a favor by trading him to the Pirates ahead of the 1978 season. That opportunity, however, would also prove to be short lived.

Before they broke camp, Pittsburgh released Martz. He could have checked on other jobs in professional baseball, but even at just 26, he was done with Organized Baseball. Two weeks later, his wife filed for divorce.

"You can read between the lines on that one if you want to," Martz said. "The hopeful gravy train ended."

It was a tumultuous time in Martz's life, and for once, baseball would not provide the therapy he needed.

"I was fed up with baseball, to be honest," Martz recalled. "I didn't make any calls to try and catch on with anybody else. I just went back to Spokane."

Looking back, Martz wishes he would have made calls to try and get into coaching, something he sees, in hindsight, as a rewarding career path in baseball.

"To this day, I work with my grandkids and I love it," Martz said. "I think I would've been a pretty good coach."

During his playing career, Martz had been slowly getting a college education using a $15,000 stipend given to him in his original pro baseball contract. After earning a bachelor's degree in math, Martz went into computer analysis and data processing, where he spent 30 years for a variety of companies, including Intel.

"That was a good thing I got out of baseball," Martz said. "I got the money to go to college. I still got a career thanks to baseball."

He still discusses his baseball career with others often. Most don't understand professional baseball, though, and that frustrates Martz to no end.

"When I talk to somebody I don't know and tell them I played minor-league baseball, they ask me why I never got to the pros," Martz said, starting to get worked up. "I've lost it a couple times when people have said that to me. It's amazing how few people know the structure of baseball. I always just tell them I spent nine years as a pro. . . . A lot of people don't understand the blood, sweat, and tears that go into this. To this day, that will upset me more than anything else in the world."

Martz retired from baseball more than 40 years ago, but the invisible battle he undertook and others' inability to acknowledge it is still one of the most frustrating things he deals with. Thanks to his own humility, his son, Gary Jr., never realized what a big deal his dad was either. It wasn't until recently that he came to understand just how rare his dad's career was.

When trying to explain his career to his son, Gary often felt like a failure, so he spared him many of the details.

"These coaches in the Portland area will say to him, 'Your old man is nuts. If I'd gotten that close, I would've given my left leg to get to the majors.'"

And that's the point: anyone who gets that close wants to take the final step of getting to the big leagues. Martz got to experience that, something only 19,000 or so have ever had the honor of doing. Making it to the major leagues helped Martz complete a life goal, but it also put him behind off the diamond.

"I felt validated professionally," Martz said of his nine-year career, which saw him play in just one major-league game. "In that regard, it was probably worth it. Financially, even family-wise, it really took a toll on me. Overall, I'd probably have to say it wasn't worth it."

Nine years that included countless hours traveling and practicing, moving from small town to small town, and he has one game in the major leagues to show for it. For Martz, it represented a life's goal accomplished, but so many others left by the wayside.

Perhaps channeling his minor-league poker nights with good friend Gorman Thomas, who led the American League in home runs in 1979 and 1981, Martz believes he actually lived up to the Mick's example in one regard.

"I always said I wanted to be the next Mickey Mantle and baseball-wise, I obviously didn't do as much as him," Martz said, beginning to laugh. "But in one regard, I think I might have done as much. He was a hell of a drinker and I think I might have been able to outdrink him."

In that department, as much as on the baseball field, it would be hard to bet against the Mick. However, Martz showed on July 8, 1975, that when it comes to baseball, crazier things have happened.

5

RAFAEL MONTALVO

April 13, 1986

Stepping onto yet another bus headed for yet another distant town, Rafael Montalvo stares out a window, thinking about everywhere he's been in his baseball career. The list stretches as long as his career has. Of all the towns, all the countries in which he has played and coached professionally, nothing is quite like his current journey: pitching coach for the Pennsylvania Road Warriors of the Atlantic League of independent ball. Montalvo's summer gig is symbolic of his overall journey; while the Road Warriors have Pennsylvania in front of their name, they have nowhere to come back to all season. The Road Warriors are the only professional baseball team in America that has no home field.

They play every single game on the road. The entire season is one big road trip. Montalvo doesn't mind. He's had to travel wherever baseball has taken him, just to get one more inning, one more pitch, one more chance to coach on a professional field. The righty reached the pinnacle, but not for long enough depending on who you ask. If you watch major-league baseball, you've likely never heard his name. If you peruse the Puerto Rican winter ball record books, you wouldn't be able to miss it.

Montalvo has been a Road Warrior in his own right, but his baseball career began very early on in Rio Piedras, Puerto Rico, where he was born and raised. Baseball is life there. Jose Oquendo and Juan Nieves, the latter of whom would go on to throw a no-hitter for the Brewers,[1] are among a couple of examples of the talent the area has produced. Baseball is a way out for the island's inhabitants, an escape from poor conditions and an opportunity to create a better life. Montalvo remembers a pivotal moment from his childhood, when he was 10 or 11 years old.

"My first baseball memory was when I got my own uniform," Montalvo said. "It was made of wool and I slept with my uniform on. I remember that, yeah, I was ready to play. I was very excited."

Montalvo and the other boys from Puerto Rico looked up to the players on AA Puerto Rico, a team that fed into the Puerto Rican national team. In the 1970s, players there were raking in around $100 a weekend. That was enough incentive for Montalvo and his teammates.

"I go, 'Wow,' that was a lot for us. When you're ten years old, you look forward to playing in that league and then after that, you look forward to playing professional baseball," Montalvo said.

Playing catcher for his team in La Cumbre, in San Juan, a couple of strokes of fortune changed the course of Montalvo's career forever. Rafy's team reached the American Amateur Baseball Congress title game in Puerto Rico. Win and they would move on to play in the championships in Memphis, Tennessee. Instead of catching, Montalvo had pitched his team into the title game that Saturday. On Sunday, without being able to pitch again, his team lost and their dreams of playing in the United States were dashed. However, Montalvo's performance on the mound the previous day earned him a second chance.

The team from Carolina he'd just lost to was allowed to pick two players from other teams in the tournament and selected him as one of those two to join them in the tournament up north. Montalvo and his Carolina teammates played three games in a single day at the tournament. He was given his orders: you will catch the first two games and pitch the third. In that third game at the Sandy Koufax Baseball Congress World Series, Montalvo nearly threw a no-hitter. He pitched well at exactly the right time. Actually, he may have pitched too well too soon.

"The scout for the Dodgers was there that day and they saw me pitch," Montalvo recalled. "From that day on, they started talking to me, but I was 14 at that time."

One must be 15 to sign an international free agent contract, and Montalvo had only recently celebrated his 14th birthday. Los Angeles wanted to sign him to a professional deal, but like so many others have learned, if you want a good thing, you must wait. Charlie Metro, a former big leaguer himself, was the Dodgers area scout in Tennessee. Unable to sign

Coach Rafael Montalvo gives the thumbs-up with the Mexican Pacific League's championship trophy, after helping lead the team to a 2019 championship, the first in franchise history. *Courtesy of Rafael Montalvo*

him right away, he connected him with Ralph Avila, a Cuban scout and legend in the Dodgers organization. He was in charge of scouting Latin America for the club. After several months, the courtship finally ended happily.

"I went back to Puerto Rico after the World Series and they started talking to me," Montalvo said. "They had to wait until the next year, because they kept following me and following me and eventually, when I turned 15, they signed me."

Before most kids have their driving learner's permit, Montalvo had signed a professional baseball contract. What is perhaps even more incredible: every single member of the Dodgers organization was sent to spring training at the same facility at that time. When 1980 spring training rolled around, in Dodgertown, there were legends of the sport, and then there were a handful of young kids, including Montalvo.

"I was 15 and I see Rick Monday, Steve Garvey, Ron Cey." Montalvo listed the names still seemingly in awe. "The biggest thing to me was everybody's in one spring training together."

Seeing these big-league stars at an age when most kids were just entering high school didn't faze Montalvo either. What may have intimidated others only strengthened his resolve.

"It was very motivating for me, because I said, 'I want to be where those guys are,'" Montalvo said. "The only thing that separated our clubhouse from the major-league clubhouse was a wall. That was it."

So close, yet so far away. The organization even shared a dining room during spring training. Every so often, Latin American big leaguers would sit with the youngsters to inspire them. Even Dodgers manager Tommy Lasorda, a fluent Spanish speaker, would sit with the kids he hoped would be with him in LA in five to six years.

"He'd come to our table and say, 'Oh, guys don't worry about it. I know you guys are really young, but you should feel comfortable here,'" Montalvo remembered. "That was great for us."

When spring training broke for the regular season, it was back to reality. By the time the rookie ball team was sent to play in Lethbridge, Alberta, in Canada, Montalvo was 16 and experiencing a bit of culture shock. A native Spanish speaker, he was trying to learn English in a place that spoke mostly French. At the time, the Dodgers organization had mandatory English language classes for Spanish speakers, so that helped, but it took a couple of years. It wasn't the language, but rather the food that made the 16-year-old Montalvo homesick, nearly 3,300 miles from where he grew up.

"I had to learn how to cook," Montalvo said with a chuckle. "I called my mom and she explained it step by step, how to start cooking rice and beans. . . . Now, I'm a great chef."

At just 16, Montalvo devised a plan to speed up his English-learning skills. He embraced his own culture as well as the culture of his teammates to try to get used to his new way of life more quickly.

"I would just tell myself, 'I don't want to live with too many Latin players,'" Montalvo recalled from his plan. "Nothing against them, I just wanted to learn English. So, I started splitting time between Latin and American players."

It worked, as Montalvo said he was fluent in English within two and a half to three years. As his English improved, so did his play. By 1983, when he was just 19 years old, Montalvo went 5–5 with a 1.55 ERA in 43 appearances out of the bullpen for Single-A Vero Beach. That season got him noticed and by 1984, at the age of 20, he had worked his way up to Triple-A, where he went 3–3 with a 4.41 ERA in 45 appearances. [2] Everything seemed to be pointing toward Montalvo cracking the big leagues in 1985, but then, as it so often does, fate stepped in the way.

One night, Montalvo and his now ex-wife were sitting in their home in Albuquerque and watching *The Bad News Bears* on TV. The scene at the Astrodome played and Rafy couldn't look away.

"I told my wife, 'One day, I'd like to play there. I want to go and play there,'" Montalvo said. Unbelievably, the next day, he got his wish. He had been traded to Houston.

He finished out the 1985 season pitching for Triple-A Tucson, making 22 appearances before heading back to Puerto Rico for yet another winter ball season. In his homeland, he was well on his way to becoming a baseball legend. By the time 1986 spring training rolled around, Montalvo, soon to be 22 years old and with six years of professional baseball experience in his back pocket, was feeling comfortable. Having a couple teammates from his winter ball team in big-league camp certainly didn't hurt.

"They were my teammates, so I felt right at home," Montalvo explained. "I was very loose, because those guys, they all know what I'm capable of doing and they would tell me all the time, they'd say, 'Hey Rafy, do the same thing that you're doing in Puerto Rico. Have fun.'"

That he did, pitching well enough to be one of two finalists for the 25th spot on the team's Opening Day roster. Everyone still in big-league camp was told to bring suits to wear after the team's final spring training game against the Twins in Orlando. They would be bused to the airport and fly straight to Houston afterward. Montalvo was assured he was going to get that final spot, but he wouldn't believe it until he saw it.

"I've got my suit on and everything, but I had this little bag with jeans, tennis shoes, and a shirt just in case they tell me I'm going down," Montalvo said. "I don't want to be suited up in the minor-league complex."

He didn't have to worry about that. The game ended; he was summoned by the coaching staff and given the life-changing news.

"They call me to the office and I'm thinking, 'Okay, well at least I'm last. At least they waited until the last day of spring training,'" Montalvo said, thinking he was being sent to the minors. Manager Hal Lanier and general manager Dick Wagner were in the room and had a very important conversation in store with their young reliever.

"Well, Rafy, we want to know where you're going to stay in Houston," Wagner said.

"What do you mean?" Montalvo replied, the moment still not sinking in.

"You made the club. We want to know where you're staying. We'll get you the hotel," Wagner said.

Montalvo couldn't believe it. The team arrived in Houston hours later, and the righty told the team he needed to step away to make a phone call.

"Remember when I told you I want to make it to this place?" he asked his wife over the phone. "I'm here."

As he walked up to the Astrodome for the first time, his first time seeing it since it was on his television set, Montalvo snapped a picture. The regular season began, and for the first time in his career, he was on a big-league roster. Six games into the season, it was finally time. Nearly 9,000 fans were at the Dome as the Astros hosted the Braves. Atlanta led 7–5, and after warming up in the bullpen for what felt like forever, the 22-year-old righty from Rio Piedras was summoned.

"People say, 'Oh, this is just another game.' No, this is the big leagues," Montalvo said. "This is all you work for in your career. . . . I was very nervous, I had butterflies in my stomach. I was shaking a little bit on the mound."

That shaking clearly didn't affect his hand-eye coordination, which was quickly tested. The very first batter he faced, Glenn Hubbard, hit a rocket right back at him, which he caught. He just stood on the mound, perhaps in shock, perhaps taking the moment in.

"Hey Rafy, throw the ball. You caught it; throw the ball. Welcome to the big leagues," third baseman Phil Garner told him.

Montalvo gave the ball to him, and they threw it around the horn. Ozzie Virgil was next, a fly out victim to left field. Trouble came when Omar Moreno got ahold of one of his pitches and drove a triple to the gap, but Montalvo was able to keep his team within two runs by getting Rafael Ramirez to ground the ball back to him for the third out. A scoreless eighth inning in the books, Montalvo was sent back out in the ninth to try to hold the Braves and give his team a chance to come back in the bottom half of the frame.

This half inning would be Montalvo's first taste of the league's indifference toward him. First up was Dale Murphy, who at this point was a five-time All-Star and had won back-to-back National League MVP Awards a few years prior. Montalvo knew he wasn't going to get the benefit of the doubt on any pitch.

"I threw pitches almost right in the middle of the plate and they were called balls," Montalvo said. Catcher Alan Ashby made a trip to the mound to explain the situation to his pitcher and calm him down.

"Don't worry about it. They're not going to call it a strike, because you're a rookie and you're pitching to one of the best hitters in the league right now," Ashby said.

Montalvo gritted his teeth and went after Murphy anyway. It was to no avail; the All-Star drew a walk. The next batter, Bob Horner, drew a walk as well. The Puerto Rican righty's day was done. It was now reliever Frank DiPino's job to strand those runners on base. He got Chris Chambliss to fly out to right field, advancing Murphy to third. Then, after Horner stole second, Billy Sample grounded out to third. DiPino was one out away from escaping the jam.

Ken Oberkfell spoiled those hopes. He singled to left, easily scoring Murphy, but Horner was gunned down at the plate, keeping the Brave lead at three. It also kept Montalvo's ERA from doubling. His final line: 1 inning pitched, 1 hit, 2 walks, 1 earned run, an ERA of 9.00.[3] All in all, not a bad day at the office for a player making his major-league debut.

Better than his performance, though, was the fact his dad got to watch him on TV.

Even in Puerto Rico, TBS broadcast Braves games, so his father was able to tune in and see his son deliver what would turn out to be the only pitches of his major-league career. He called his parents after the game, and despite the short appearance, his dad knew all his hard work had paid off.

"I only pitched an inning or whatever, but he was so very proud of me."

The Astros got on a roll and eventually, when a couple of veterans returned to the club, Montalvo was sent back down to Triple-A Tucson. He watched from afar as the franchise he belonged to kept on winning. Houston won the NL West with a 96–66 record. Had the Astros beaten the Mets in the NLCS, the Bill Buckner boot would have never happened. As his bonus share for the team winning the division, Montalvo was sent a $500 check.

"I remember I got that check and I was like, 'Wow, I was there for just a few weeks,'" Montalvo said. "Imagine when I get there for the whole year."

He would have to keep imagining. That solitary "inning or whatever" would be the only one. Tucson was the only American city he played professional baseball in for the next two seasons. Despite going 17–5 with an ERA hovering around 4.00 in those two seasons, control issues continued to keep him from the big leagues. He walked nearly as many as he struck out in 1987 and had less than a 3:2 strikeout-to-walk ratio in 1988. His inability to get back to the major leagues wasn't for lack of effort, and as so many others have had the unfortunate honor of learning, it may not have been for lack of results either.

"I know in my mind and my body, I put everything into it," Montalvo said, "but it wasn't up to me."

That didn't keep him from questioning why he wasn't earning calls to the majors despite his relatively strong performance.

"I asked what it would take for me to make the club and they said, 'You need to get some experience,'" Montalvo said. "How do you think I'm going to get experience in the major leagues if you don't let me play there?"

Heading into the 1989 season, Montalvo was a free agent for the first time and his years in Houston were over. Seemingly stuck in Triple-A, he opted to sign with the Indians, who offered him a split minor- and major-league contract. The money was good, so he put his name on the dotted line. Two days before the regular season was set to begin, the Indians sent Montalvo down to the minors. The next day, they released him. Still just 25 years old, Montalvo was confused.

"Why did you release me?" Montalvo asked.

"You're going to make too much money," was the reply Cleveland gave him, according to Montalvo.

"Well, you're the guy who offered me the contract. I wasn't asking for that money," a stunned Montalvo reasoned.

With so little time before the season, Montalvo didn't play Organized Baseball in the States in 1989. Instead, he played in Mexico. During that winter ball season in Puerto Rico, his manager was Maximino Oliveras. It just so happened that Oliveras was also the Triple-A manager for the California Angels. After having a good year in Puerto Rico, Montalvo was signed by the Angels. Future Angels and Mariners general manager Bill Bavasi, California's farm director at the time, was the one to give Montalvo the nod in the end.

Montalvo was given a chance to make the Angels Opening Day roster in 1990, but he wasn't able to do so. Seemingly, he was the 13th pitcher on a team that would take 12 into the regular season. He posted a solid year in '90, registering a 2.74 ERA, the lowest at the Triple-A level in his career. Bavasi was impressed.

"Before the season was over, Bill Bavasi came and signed me for the next year," Montalvo said. "He told me I did a great job and did everything they expected from me. . . . 'We want to sign you again, plus we want to invite you to big-league camp,'" Montalvo remembered Bavasi telling him.

A second year with the Angels, a second chance to once again make a big-league roster four years after his debut. Montalvo's play dropped off sharply, though, and he split time between Double-A and Triple-A after not making the team's big-league roster out of camp. His ERA ballooned to 6.00 in 47 appearances. Knowing he wasn't going to get an immediate chance at a big-league roster after a season like that and knowing he needed to make a grown-up decision at 27 years old, Montalvo decided professional baseball in America wasn't the way to give his family the best life possible.

"Baseball is everything for me. I do whatever I can to play, but there has to be a point in your life where you have to take care of your family," Montalvo said. "At that point, I had kids, I just said, 'I have to make money.'"

Playing in the minor leagues was not a way to do that then, and it still isn't today. Montalvo estimates that after taxes, he brought home between $18,000 and $20,000 for playing in the minor leagues. In Mexico, for six months of work, he would make between $30,000 and $35,000, tax-free. At that point in his life, it was a no-brainer. Thus, he played professionally in Mexico between 1992 and 1994. However, when professional baseball players went on strike during the 1994 season, stretching into the spring of 1995, Montalvo became a controversial figure. Nine years after making his major-league debut, he crossed the picket line to try to play for the Dodgers, the team that had signed him half his life ago.

Before that, he had played for the most legendary Latin American baseball team of all time. Montalvo and his teammates called the 1995 San Juan team the "Dream Team" and for good reason. With Major League Baseball players on strike, many stars wanted to play in the Caribbean. An influx of talent poured into Puerto Rico and onto Montalvo's San Juan team in particular. Here's how that San Juan team's lineup card was filled out:

1B Carmelo Martinez
2B Roberto Alomar
3B Carlos Baerga
SS Rey Sanchez
LF Juan Gonzalez
CF Bernie Williams
RF Ruben Sierra
C Carlos Delgado
DH Edgar Martinez
Injured: C Ivan Rodriguez

Between those 11 guys, there are three Hall of Fame plaques, 50 All-Star appearances, seven World Series titles, and 2,587 home runs. *USA Today Baseball Weekly* called this collection of players the "Team of the Century." And Montalvo was among its members, playing with the game's stars during MLB's most trying offseason ever.

"In my opinion, we're never going to see a team like that again," Montalvo said, still marveling at the assembly of talent that San Juan team had.

LA made it hard for replacement players like Montalvo to stay away by the time spring rolled around. They offered by far the most lucrative offer to replacement players of any team in the big leagues. Class-A players would receive a minimum $3,000-a-month salary, Double-A players would receive a minimum $5,000-a-month salary, and Triple-A players would receive a minimum $7,000-a-month salary.

"I said, 'Guys, if you don't want to play, I do want to play in the big leagues,'" Montalvo said. "They offered me too much money and I did it for my family. I didn't do it to embarrass you guys."

Plus, it had been nearly four years since Montalvo had played in the league for which he once had such grand ambitions. All factors added up, it was far too much to pass on.

"I wanted to go back to the States and play. This gave me a chance to do that."

As Bob Nightengale noted in the *Los Angeles Times* in his March 2, 1995, story, a Yankees-Dodgers spring training game was expected to spark protestors to show up from far and wide.

> A police escort will await on the outer limits of Ft. Lauderdale. And security guards will escort the team into the clubhouse. . . . Who cares if the pitching match-up is Rafael Montalvo vs. the Yankees' Frank Eufenia, neither of whom has pitched in the big leagues since 1986? . . . "People are talking a lot about it," Montalvo said, "but I'm not afraid. If we go down there, and we have to stay on the bus, we'll stay on the bus. If it's real bad and we have to go home, we'll go home. I've been through some scary situations in Mexico, but I don't think the people in this country will throw rocks or bottles. Police will be there to protect us, anyway."[4]

As the spring drew on and it appeared replacement players would have to open the regular season on big-league teams, Montalvo said the Dodgers would be thanking them for putting the team in first place by the time they got back. Star catcher Mike Piazza didn't hold back his criticism of Montalvo and the other replacement players, as he later recalled in his book *Long Shot*:

Some of the replacement players—mainly, a pitcher named Rafael Montalvo, who had pitched one inning for the Astros back in 1986 and hadn't played organized ball in the States for three years—were saying things like they were going to have us five games in first place by the time we got back and we'd probably want to thank them. . . . Does someone really think we'll be rooting for these guys? What do they think we'll do if we win it, give them a playoff share? Do they want rings? We'll give them rings all right—made of tin.[5]

Piazza's strong words were emblematic of the general sentiment of actual major leaguers toward replacement players at the time. In fact, part of ongoing negotiations with owners included the fact that any regular-season games the replacement players played in would not count in the standings once the regulars came back. Montalvo saw things a different way.

"They gave you an opportunity to make money. I don't want to take your job," he said. "You guys gave it away. . . . I did it for my family, because those big-league players aren't going to pay my bills and they don't want to play. They make millions of dollars and don't want to play? I want to play baseball," Montalvo continued. "I don't have anything against those players and I respect those guys a lot. I do. . . . There were some that understood it. Not everyone."

Of course, Montalvo and the other replacement players never actually suited up in the big leagues, but he did get a nice paycheck for playing in Triple-A that year. He actually had one of his more impressive seasons, going 3–5 with a 2.65 ERA in 49 appearances. At 31 years old, though, no major-league teams were giving him a serious look. After the 1995 season, Montalvo added a fourth country to his list of places he'd played baseball professionally.

While playing in Mexico in 1996, Montalvo was teammates with Jose Cano, whose 13-year-old son, Robinson, would soon become a household name. Cano planned to play in Taiwan after the Mexican League season was over, and he heard that another team needed a pitcher. Just as Maximino Oliveras had done with the Angels, Cano advocated for Montalvo. When offered a contract to play in Taiwan in 1996, Montalvo responded in a way that would come to define his career in professional baseball: "Why not?"

"It was the end of August and I had just come back from Mexico," Montalvo said. "I was in my house for two weeks, packed my stuff and I went to Taiwan."

After three years in Taiwan, Montalvo returned to the Western Hemisphere. Upon returning, one of his baseball mentors and a man he described as one of his "baseball dads," Ellie Rodriguez, asked him if he was interested in playing independent ball back in the States.

"Why not?"

He joined the Atlantic City Surf as a starting pitcher for the 1999 season, his 13th professional season in the States spread across 19 years.

"They offered me a job in Atlantic City, so how can I say no to that deal?" Montalvo said.

If signing Montalvo was a gamble, it paid off. He went 10–8 with a 3.89 ERA in 24 starts in independent ball. It was the final season he would play in the United States. Ellie Rodriguez urged Montalvo to play at least one more year after the solid season he had, but he had played enough, at least in the States. While playing in his 21st Puerto Rican League season, he was told by one of his coaches, Edwin Rodriguez, that the Tampa Bay Devil Rays organization was looking for a bilingual minor-league pitching coach. Rodriguez himself was a scout and coach with Tampa.

"What would you think if I gave them your name?" Rodriguez asked.

Montalvo was interested. He was then contacted by farm director Tom Foley, who interviewed him for the job. In a nutshell, their conversation went a little something like this:

"I'm looking for a bilingual pitching coach," Foley said.

"Well, I'm here," Montalvo responded.

"If you want it, the job is yours," Foley told the nearly retired right-handed pitcher.

"Why not?"

Montalvo joined the Devil Rays in spring training 2000. When he arrived in uniform, former teammates were very confused.

"Oh, are you here to pitch?" they asked.

"No, I'm your coach," he replied.

"No way, Rafy!" His former teammates were coming to realize Montalvo was now their boss.

"Yeah, I just got a new job. I'm done with baseball," Montalvo said. "It was funny, because they thought that I was ready to pitch."

They weren't entirely wrong. Even while coaching in the Devil Rays' organization, Rafael Montalvo continued to play in Puerto Rico for a couple more years. After all, he had some records to break. He kept going back, 23 seasons in total, in order to break the Puerto Rican record for most career pitching appearances and most wins in a single decade. He broke both and was then named to Puerto Rico's All-Half Century team, putting him among the best to play baseball in Puerto Rico's 50 years of Organized Ball.

"To be one of the pitchers on that team, I was very, very proud of that," Montalvo said.

When the San Juan team moved to nearby Carolina, they built a brand-new stadium. Montalvo was living in Carolina and convinced the team's owner to let him pitch the first game ever played there. How can you argue with a player who's been with the franchise for more than two decades? He was the team's starting pitcher when Carolina Stadium opened. When Montalvo decided to retire in 2002, he again made a request that he be allowed to pitch against Caguas on the road and leave the game on his own terms. Of course, the veteran was allowed to do so.

He threw a complete game shutout, and his team won 2–0. With that, his professional playing career was over. Now, his sole focus was on coaching. The next decade of his career was spent with Tampa Bay, where he worked with pitchers like James Shields and David Price, who he later got to see pitch in the franchise's first and only World Series in 2008, when he was still with the organization. He will still see the guys that he calls "his pitchers" from time to time.

"It's very satisfying for me that I got to work with them and every time I see them, they just say hi," Montalvo said. "I don't need much. That's the only thing that I want when they see me, for them to say hi to me and shake my hand."

They have lived out the career Montalvo always dreamed of having himself. He walked away from baseball in the United States several times, but he still wonders why he never got a real shot to prove himself.

"I was so young. I was happy to make the major leagues at that time," Montalvo reflected. "But I wondered too what would've happened if I would've stayed longer."

It's the wondering, the what-ifs that eat away at nearly every player who failed to sustain a major-league career. Unlike most, Montalvo was able to play professionally elsewhere for over two decades. In that time, his legacy in baseball became one that saw him establish himself as a legend in Puerto Rico. He also befriended some of the most talented ballplayers to ever come out of the Caribbean.

"I see Robbie Alomar like a professional player and a Hall of Famer, but to me, he's just a friend that I can call. I have his phone number and I can just call him," Montalvo said. "When Edgar Martinez was selected to the Hall of Fame, I have his phone number, so I was able to tell him congratulations. . . . We shared a lot of good memories, those guys and me. That's why baseball has been so good to me."

So, as the bus departs, Montalvo a passenger yet again on his 40-year journey in professional baseball, he's continued to prove during all that time that even without a home field, the destination doesn't much matter. As long as there's dirt in the shape of a diamond, he can make a livelihood, and a home.

6

JEFF BANISTER

July 23, 1991

Born the son of a football coach, Jeff Banister was destined to be a star on the gridiron. Then, life threw him a curveball. As a five-year-old, Banister was sent to a baseball camp in Enid, Oklahoma—his home state—and he was hooked on the sport. His love for the game grew from there through Little League and into his teenage years.

Before he went to school, he would go with his dad, Bob, to another school where Bob, in addition to coaching football, coached baseball. Jeff would observe all the coaches in the room. The smell of coffee and cigarettes would fill the air as the coaches broke down game film. He saw how the coaches taught and motivated their players. At a young age, he thought that might be fun someday.

Banister started establishing himself as a force to be reckoned with at La Marque High School in Texas. Playing high school baseball put him on a stage bigger than most as he played against tougher competition than most of the rest of the country.

As his development continued, Banister caught a bad break. He injured his right ankle during his sophomore season and the injury was slow to heal. The injury may, in fact, have saved his life.

"Laying in a hospital bed and not being able to play and dreaming of being back out on the field was probably one of the true drivers of why I'm so passionate about this game," Banister said.

Doctors ran tests to see why his injury was healing so slowly. Their answer came back: Jeff had bone cancer.

At 16 years old, Banister was in for the fight of his life, also diagnosed with osteomyelitis, the same bone disease that plagued Mickey Mantle. Banister was trapped in solitude, a three-by-three window his only glimpse into the outside world.

"I could barely see the sunshine," Banister said. "I would just dream about when I would be able to get back out and play baseball."

Doctors advised the best way to keep the osteomyelitis from spreading to the rest of his leg was to amputate. Banister refused to have his leg amputated, because he still had dreams of playing baseball at a high level. Seven surgeries were performed on the 16-year-old to save his leg, while ensuring the osteomyelitis didn't spread.

For a long time, Banister did not fully understand the severity of the situation. It was not until he began to read his relatives' body language that he figured he was in some real trouble.

"Friends and family members would visit me in the hospital room," Banister said. "I never saw smiles. Both my mom and dad would cry a lot."

Jeff Banister stands on first base, taking signs, after singling in his only career plate appearance for the Pirates in 1991. *Courtesy of MLB*

His aunt—his father's sister—died of cancer while Banister was in the hospital fighting his own form of the deadly disease. His dad skipped his sister's funeral to be at his son's bedside to ensure he won his own fight.

Hardly old enough to drive a car, Banister continued to use baseball as his light at the end of the tunnel. It was never certain that the tunnel would end in anything but darkness; however, after a successful fight, the end of the tunnel did eventually come into view, lit by his love for the game. By his senior year of high school, he was recovered, cancer-free, and able to compete again. His cancer fight served as a motivator for the rest of his playing career.

"I didn't want to feel that absence again, so I wanted to get back out on the field," Banister said.

Without four full years to show scouts what he could do at La Marque High School in Texas, Banister opted to attend Lee College, a junior college in Baytown, Texas, less than 30 minutes from his hometown. In 1983, less than two years after beating cancer, Banister was playing in a fall league game, the final game of the season.

He was not supposed to play in the game at all, but a Yankees scout had asked his coach if he could see him play behind the plate at catcher. His coach obliged and told Banister he would play just five innings behind the plate. Banister agreed to catch.

It was a beautiful Sunday afternoon with nothing but blue skies over Texas. With a runner on third base in the fifth inning, Banister was a couple of outs from ending his day. The batter on the opposing team hit a shallow fly ball to right field. Banister can still vividly recall what happened next, pain in his voice, as if it's happening all over again.

"The outfielder caught it flat footed, a right-handed thrower threw the ball in and the ball tailed up the third-base line," Banister said. "I knew I was going to have to try and glove it and tag the runner on the way by and thought the runner would try to go around me."

The ball continued to tail, and the runner from third continued to chug down the line, with no sign he was going to change his path to the plate.

"I made the decision to go to my knees and block the ball and try to sweep tag and when the ball hit my glove and I looked up, the runner was coming straight down the line," Banister said. "The runner tried to jump over the top of me and his knee hit the top of my head and shoved my skull and three vertebrae straight down and they just exploded outward."

"After that, there was a lot of nothing."

Banister lay motionless on the field, the top of his head split open by the force of the runner's knee. A man of faith, Banister remembers a distinct lack of feeling, a divine experience. When he came to, he was being cradled by an assistant coach. Everyone was concerned by the gash on the top of his head.

His father made it down to field level and saw the damage. He realized what everyone else did: his son needed to be rushed to the hospital.

"You're in trouble, aren't you?" his father asked.

"Yeah, I am," Banister responded.

An ambulance was called, and after what felt like an eternity, Banister was transported to a local hospital and was immediately put in traction. His most chilling memory from the day came when his mom helped him in the hospital:

"I remember my mother—I was still in uniform and I still had all that baseball field on my jersey—she cut my uniform off me," Banister said. "They sedated me. The next day, I got the news."

The tough-as-nails catcher who had beaten cancer in his adolescence was now paralyzed from the neck down. Doctors weren't sure he'd ever be able to walk again. Banister was confined to a hospital bed and the close confines of his room for the second time in his life.

"There was a ton of fear. . . . Then, I thought, 'Okay, this is not permanent. We're going to beat this.'" Banister said. "It was just another obstacle I had to overcome."

The 18-year-old competitor may have been naive in his thinking at the time, but he ended up being right: it was not permanent. After nearly two weeks, he began to regain feeling, a sign he would not be paralyzed forever. Rigorous physical therapy followed, and Banister was eventually discharged.

The stocky catcher entered the hospital weighing 225 pounds. He left weighing just 139. His body had been ravaged. Almost all of his muscle was gone. He spent the entire 1984 season relearning how to walk.

Unbelievably, Banister had recovered fully by the time the 1985 season rolled around and played the best baseball of his young life. He was named a Junior College All-American in 1985 at Lee College, which opened the door for him to transfer to a bigger program. Again, he didn't look beyond the wide reaches of Texas.

Banister chose the University of Houston. During his 1986 season there, he drew the attention of Buzzy Keller, a scout for the Pittsburgh

Pirates. Keller saw something special in Banister, a young man who had already overcome more than most do in a lifetime.

"He was willing to look past the injuries and the risk of drafting a guy that had been through so much," Banister said. "He looked at the talent level and thought there was a little more in my makeup and desire."

The evening of the 1986 MLB draft, Banister had gone out for the night. It was not yet a televised event, nor was it one that generated the publicity it does now. He arrived home to see something his mother had put in the yard.

"My mom had put up a sign in the yard saying what round I was drafted and by whom," Banister said.

The sign said: "Pittsburgh Pirates, 25th round."

He signed with Pittsburgh, officially beginning what would become a journey spanning three decades with the franchise. His first stop on the long road was Watertown, New York, where he joined the Pirates' Low-A affiliate. In 41 games, he hit just .145 with 27 strikeouts and four extra-base hits. His introduction to professional baseball was a rough one.

As he had his entire life to that point, though, he fought through adversity to make himself better. The 1987 season saw him hit .254 in 101 games, and his OPS jumped from .402 to .693.[1] He was playing for the Single-A Macon Pirates by this time. The 1987 season would also be the last season he'd play in front of his dad.

Bob Banister died of a heart attack on January 13, 1988, at 48 years old. Banister's grandfather passed away three weeks later. Just as he was trying to establish himself as a professional ballplayer, tragedy once again threatened to get in the way. His next two seasons were spent at Double-A Harrisburg, where he continued to struggle, hitting no higher than .259.

In 1991, he was ready to turn the corner. Having played just 12 career games in Triple-A, Banister, Pirates pocket schedule in hand, called his wife, Karen.

"I was joking around and I said, 'Hey, if I get called up by July 23rd, you know where the Pirates are coming the next day, right?'" There was a pause on the other end of the line.

"I had a pen in my hand circling the date on this calendar and I said, 'We'll be in Houston and we'll get to see each other.' We laughed about it," Banister recalled.

Neither of them questioned Banister's talent or desire. That isn't why they were laughing. The 1991 Pittsburgh Pirates were simply loaded.

They had Don Slaught, an all-star and Gold Glover behind the plate, Banister's position. They had a young Barry Bonds. Expectations were high, and many thought the Bucs should compete for a World Series title. It was not the place for a fringe player to catch his break.

He did get one step closer, though, to within an injury of reaching the big leagues. Banister was optioned to Triple-A Buffalo for the start of the 1991 season. On July 22, just before midnight, he and roommate Jeff Richardson were packing for a road trip to Oklahoma City and watching ESPN.

They watched baseball highlights, including the Pirates game. There was no mention of the injury Don Slaught sustained. As the two men continued to pack, the phone at their apartment began to ring. Richardson picked up.

"The phone is for you. It's T.C. [Buffalo manager Terry Collins]," Richardson told Banister.

"We used to do that all the time and would joke with each other," Banister said. "The phone would ring late at night, and we'd jokingly say, 'It's T.C. and you just got called up,' so at the time, I was like, 'Yeah, okay. Ha, ha, ha.'" At this point, Banister was a man with no reason to believe that he'd find any good news on the other end of a telephone.

Richardson eventually got Banister to pick up the phone and it was, in fact, Collins on the other end. Banister greeted his manager.

"Hello?" Banister said.

"Hey, it's T.C. How long have you been waiting for this call?" Collins asked.

"I don't know. What's up?" a perplexed Banister asked, continuing to think he was the subject of an elaborate prank.

"Don Slaught got hurt. You're going to the big leagues tomorrow," Collins said.

"Get the heck out of here, who is this?" Banister asked, still wondering when the joke would finally be up.

He turned to Richardson. "C'mon, who is this? What kind of joke is this?"

Banister got back on the phone with Collins, who tried once again to make it very clear how serious he was about the fact Banister was being called up.

"Hey, Sluggo got hurt," Collins said. "You're going up tomorrow. I don't know how long you're going to be there, but they need a catcher and you're the guy."

The third time was the charm. Banister finally allowed himself to realize there was no joke: he would be in a major-league uniform within 24 hours.

"At that moment, my entire body felt numb," Banister remembered. "I didn't know whether to feel excited, scared, or overjoyed. I remember thinking immediately that I needed to call somebody, but I had nobody to call."

His wife and mother were on their way to Oklahoma City to see him play the following day. It was going to be the first time he'd seen his wife since spring training. His joking prophecy about being called up before July 23 had been shockingly accurate. He had a ticket waiting for him at the airport the following day.

"It was the first time I ever flew first class," Banister said. "Buffalo to Pittsburgh is a pretty short flight, but it was first class nonetheless."

He got to Pittsburgh without a sports coat. The 27-year-old bought one after he arrived and was able to finally call his wife and mom and let them know what was going on.

"There were a lot of tears and a lot of joy," Banister said. "Then, I realized I was going to get to the ballpark and there were going to be no family members there."

Pittsburgh was set to host the Braves at Three Rivers Stadium that night. Banister got to the stadium as early as you'd expect a rookie to arrive for his first game in the bigs. A security guard let him into the clubhouse and locker room, which was still dark. The only source of light was the exit sign. His jersey was already hanging up in his locker.

"I thought it was the coolest thing ever to see a major-league uniform with your name on it," Banister said. "Then, they took me upstairs to sign my contract. . . . I had never seen a comma in any one single paycheck or contract before that," Banister said, recalling how he'd signed for nearly six figures.

"I used to play this game for fun as a kid and used to ride my bike to the sandlot," Banister said. "Now I was getting paid, I believe $97,000 to play a game that I loved to play."

Rain started to come down on July 23 in Pittsburgh. Banister was unable to take batting practice on the field during his first night in the major leagues. Banister faced a whirlwind of questions from droves of reporters armed with the knowledge of his incredible backstory. It was his first experience being interviewed by a reporter in anything but a one-on-one setting.

Banister was on the bench that night, a backup catcher. Pittsburgh powered its way to a 10–3 lead by the seventh inning. With such a big lead, starting pitcher Doug Drabek had no reason to stay in the game. Banister was in the bullpen when the phone rang. He was told he would pinch-hit for Drabek, a fellow University of Houston Cougar.

"I get down to the dugout and I can't find my bat or anything," Banister said. "I just grabbed my helmet, grabbed a bat, which turned out to be Cecil Espy's bat and went up to the plate. . . . I just remember my heart pounding," Banister said. "I couldn't feel my legs." The lack of sensation was more welcome compared to the last time.

The pinch-hitter can still run through the pitch progression of his at bat vividly. On the first pitch, he was intent on trying to hit it out of the ballpark. He swung and missed. The second offering to him buzzed the tower, coming in just under his jaw line. Pitch no. 3 was a slider, and he put a good swing on it.

"I hit it in the hole and it seemed like every single step down the line took forever until I hit the bag and knew I was safe," Banister said. "I felt my foot and I could hear the pop of the glove and I saw the umpire throw out his hands to say I was safe and it was just a whirlwind of emotions."

His shot between the shortstop and third baseman on the left side resulted in an infield single. Jeff Banister had notched a hit in the major leagues, wearing a uniform once worn by the likes of Clemente and Stargell. As he triumphantly stood on first base, he thought back on all of the people who had helped him to overcome a lifetime fraught with adversity.

"I wanted all of them to be able to experience it and understand the appreciation that I knew what it had taken," Banister said. "I didn't get there by myself."

Luckily, Banister soaked it in, because he would never take a big-league field as a player again after that night. In his only at bat, he got his single, giving him a career batting average of 1.000. As soon as Slaught returned from injury, Banister was optioned back to Triple-A Buffalo. He admits to playing angry after getting sent back down, wishing he had gotten an extended period of time in the big leagues.

"When you achieve your dream or you climb Mount Everest and all of a sudden, you have to come back down, it's just a memory," Banister said. "What's next? You always need that next step. I didn't have that next step."

After injuring his elbow and missing the entire 1992 season, Banister's career was slowly winding to a close. In what served as a swan song for his playing career and foreshadowed his coaching career, Banister was a player-coach for the Double-A Carolina Mudcats in 1993, playing in just eight games. During this transition, Banister learned a fundamental truth about the game, one which he still shares with his players:

"What we do is fleeting; it doesn't last forever," Banister said. "We don't necessarily get to choose how long it lasts."

The same is true of coaching, where it's even harder to reach the game's highest level as an MLB manager.

"It was never my intent when I started managing that I was going to be a major-league manager," Banister said. "The realization kicks in: 'This may be harder to do than being a player.' When you play, you're hanging on your own at bats and plays. When you're a manager, you have 25 to 40 players to worry about."

From 1994 to 1998, Banister served as a manager in the Pirates' farm system. He transitioned into being the major-league field coordinator between 1999 and 2002. From there, he was named minor-league field coordinator, a position he held from 2003 to 2010. In July 2010, he was brought onto the Pirates' big-league staff as the bench coach. After paying more than 25 seasons of dues, Banister was back on a major-league bench, this time as a coach.

When he thinks back to that time in his life, he recalls a conversation with his wife.

"There was a point in time where my wife, Karen, and I were sitting in the back of our house and we looked at each other and said, 'If this is as good as it gets, are we okay? Are we good?' The answer was yes," Banister said. "We made an impact on a lot of different people in a lot of different areas."

He got to see countless players he coached and mentored live out their major-league dreams, continuations of a dream realized but not fully captured by Banister himself. After the 2010 season, Banister was asked to interview for the Pirates' managerial opening. It came down to him and former Colorado Rockies manager Clint Hurdle. Pittsburgh hired Hurdle.

After 25 coaching seasons, Banister was instead tabbed the permanent bench coach.

"I was blessed to spend four great years with Clint, where he shaped, molded, and mentored me," Banister said.

He spent the next four seasons as the Pirates' bench coach before he again generated serious interest in his ability as a manager at the MLB level. He interviewed with the Houston Astros for their managerial opening in 2014 after Bo Porter was fired. It would have been a homecoming, but Houston hired A. J. Hinch instead.

"It was a little bit of a letdown with it being my hometown team and them starting to generate some excitement," Banister remembered.

Another team from Texas was waiting in the wings, however; as Banister prepared for the Pirates' wild-card playoff game with the San Francisco Giants, he was told Texas Rangers general manager Jon Daniels had called, wanting to gauge his interest in the Rangers' managerial opening. His mind on the playoff game the following day, Banister said he could give Daniels 45 minutes to an hour of his time.

"It was a great conversation. We really hit it off on the phone and then my mind starts racing about Texas," Banister said. "It's back home. Then, I think about the 29 years I was with Pittsburgh."

As the Rangers possibility stirred in his mind, Banister was torn. He turned his attention back to the Pirates' playoff game. Pittsburgh lost to San Francisco, that season's eventual World Series champion, 8–0, in a game dominated by Madison Bumgarner. Jeff and Karen loaded up their truck and headed back home to Texas.

"We got about halfway home and I got another phone call from Jon Daniels and he asked me if I'd be able to come into Arlington to interview," Banister said. "So, the whole excitement and anticipation started all over again."

It was clear early on that Banister's heavy analytics background meshed with the front office interested in hiring him. His heart still belonged to the Pirates, but after visiting Globe Life Park for the first time for his interview, he saw the chance at a new beginning.

"They were very open minded, smart, brilliant, baseball people who shared some of the same thoughts and mind-sets about the game, the management, the people," Banister said. "I knew then that it could be a great place that I could bring my family and we could start the whole managerial career."

On October 16, 2014, Banister was named the next manager of the Texas Rangers. In spring training of his first season as a big-league manager, Banister faced yet another test.

"I didn't tell anybody," Banister said. "I just wanted it to go away. I was in denial. Scared? Yes. Stubborn? Yes."

Banister felt miserable, and his ankle was swelling. He saw streaks of discoloration on his skin that he recognized. He feared his cancer had returned in time to rob him of his chance at managing a major-league team. Without telling anyone what was going on, he fought through the pain. With Opening Day looming, Banister needed relief.

Texas hosted two exhibition games in Arlington after spring training before the regular season began. Banister managed in the first one. He doesn't remember anything from the game because he was so sick. The following day, he was sent home. After a visit to the doctor, he was believed to have a bad infection. He was given antibiotics, which slowly improved his condition.

"It started getting better, so I flew to Oakland and I was able to start my managerial career," Banister said. "Day one in Oakland was rough. I felt like crap. I remember very little of it. I got better the next day and continued to get better every day after that."

Texas got off to a rough start in 2015, but they finished strong, going 33–17 in their final 50 games to win the American League West title. In his rookie managerial season, he was named the American League Manager of the Year.

As someone who had just scratched the surface at the big-league level, jumping over enormous hurdles to do so, Banister is able to provide unique insight to his players, who live out his MLB dream every day.

"I tell young guys all the time: you have to have dreams and goals of getting to the big leagues, but just getting there should never be the no. 1 goal," Banister said. "For me, just getting there was the no. 1 goal. I set that sight at a high peak, yet I didn't have the next step in my mind for, 'Okay, I made it to the big leagues, what next?'"

A manager who knows what all his players had to do to get there (and then some), Banister doesn't allow them to lower their sights, to quell their ambitions.

"Never settle, because the day you settle for what you do is the day that you get knocked down a peg or two on what you will achieve,"

Banister said. "What my players can learn from my story is, 'Don't ever quit.' You can't replace playing, so don't ever quit. You're never out."

There were numerous occasions where Banister could have been out. He could have been out of baseball, out of mobility, out of life on this earth. Instead of giving up, he sprinted down the line just as he did on July 23, 1991, in a Pittsburgh Pirates uniform as he earned every inch of his one career hit.

On April 10, 2018, infielder Isiah Kiner-Falefa made his major-league debut for the Rangers. Banister, having been there nearly 27 years earlier, pulled his rookie aside.

"Don't miss the first pitch of the game," Banister told Kiner-Falefa. "Don't miss the national anthem. Don't miss the crowd noise. Don't miss the smell of the ballpark." He passed on a sentiment he'd learned first-hand decades before, and which he'd seen played out before his eyes on countless occasions since:

"You only get one opportunity for one first time and you never know if that will be the only time."

7

STEPHEN LARKIN

September 27, 1998

Athletes were growing on trees in the Larkin household in the 1970s and 1980s; Robert and Shirley Larkin raised their oldest daughter, Mary, and their three other boys Barry, Michael, and Byron to be competitors at the highest level. As a result, competition became the way of life in their Cincinnati home. Eight years after Byron, their youngest of five children, Stephen, was born.

As many youngest siblings are, Stephen was thrown into the fire early, most often playing sports with kids twice his size and age. If the sun was shining, the Larkins were outside playing football, basketball, or baseball.

"Our dad never really worked on the lawn, because he knew we were just going to tear it up," Stephen Larkin said.

They would use soda cartons for bases, killing the grass that Robert eventually gave up on maintaining. It was this constant competition that drove all four boys to dream of playing sports at a high level. Being the youngest, Stephen got to watch from afar as his three older brothers all saw those dreams realized.

"I had a coach in every sport," Larkin said. "Barry was playing baseball, Michael was playing college football, and Byron was playing basketball. Our sister, Mary, who's a doctor now, was like my tutor. She was everybody's tutor and counselor. She kept us all in check and ran things."

They had another coach in their mother, Shirley.

"Every game, the voice you hear coming out of the crowd is hers. I'm talking either way, good or bad," Larkin said. "If you did well, she was

Stephen Larkin poses with his mother, Shirley, one of his many sources of inspiration. *Courtesy of Stephen Larkin*

yelling for you and if you did poorly, she let you have it. She was someone you could hear coming from a mile away."

It was this encouragement and passion that helped fuel the Larkins to athletic success. Both she and Robert pushed their children to pursue the dreams they had.

As Stephen grew up, his three brothers, all separated by less than two years in age, started leaving the house. When Stephen was just nine, Barry was picked in the second round of the MLB draft by the Cincinnati Reds. Wanting to get an education and move even higher in the draft, Barry attended the University of Michigan for three seasons. In the 1985 MLB draft, the Reds took him again, this time fourth overall. [1]

When Stephen was 11, Byron began a four-year basketball career at Xavier University in Cincinnati, where he would become a second-team All-American. He could've played Division I football as well; he was an All-American on the gridiron in high school. [2] Michael was playing linebacker for Notre Dame at the same time, which made the pilgrimage to Notre Dame Stadium a staple of that portion of Stephen's childhood. [3]

Right as middle school began, Stephen was on his own in the Larkin household. However, with his siblings still relatively close by, he was able to continue to receive that coaching as he tried to live up to the family's already strong athletic legacy.

"When it came time to do what I was doing, they were right there supporting me like I had been doing all the time for them growing up," Larkin said.

Stephen seemed to be following in the footsteps of his older brothers, putting together two solid seasons at Cincinnati's Archbishop Moeller High School on the baseball field. His junior year would be a big one; scouts would be more interested in him as he approached the end of his high school career. Before his junior year began, he was getting in some work with the rest of the players during a team activity.

"We were doing early-season workouts and we were running sprints," Larkin recalled. "I passed out one morning."

Larkin didn't think much of it. He went home and talked to his mom about what had happened. They discussed what could have caused him to pass out. He had raced out of the house at six in the morning to get to the workout, so each came to the reasonable conclusion that his fatigue and lack of sleep were to blame.

"We were all athletes, so I went back the next morning," Larkin said. "Everything was good for offseason workouts and then I went to see a cardiologist about a month later."

That cardiologist delivered crushing news: he saw something in Larkin he had never seen before, so he couldn't clear him to play high school sports. The diagnosis was hypertrophic cardiomyopathy, a rare heart condition. The condition is incredibly rare for someone Stephen's age at the time of diagnosis. It is defined as a disease that makes it hard for the heart to pump blood; it often goes undiagnosed. The most common symptoms include shortness of breath, chest pains, and an irregular heartbeat.

Larkin didn't know what to do with news like that. He was supposed to be following in the footsteps of his older brothers, but now a wrench had been thrown into his plan and his life. Doctors told Larkin that continuing to play baseball could potentially be fatal. He could die on the field.

"It was life changing, because this guy is telling me I'm not going to be an athlete anymore," Larkin said. "I thought my athletic career might be over. That thought crossed my mind for a second, but then I said, 'There's no way.' This is what we do. I've watched them do it my whole life, now it's my turn to do it."

However, Larkin was not allowed to play any sports for Archbishop Moeller High School after his sophomore year. The high school took the medical information on Stephen and went to the archdiocese of Ohio. Rather than risk Larkin fainting again, or worse, dying on the field, they decided not to let him play sports for the high school anymore.

With the high school team being the only way for Larkin to play football, he also had to give up on his football dream, which Barry said was his brother's best sport. Playing a contact sport like football was out of the question with hypertrophic cardiomyopathy.

"I still went to and graduated from Moeller and still played summer ball hoping someone would give me a look while playing summer baseball," Larkin said.

He played his summer ball for Midland, a team based in Cincinnati. Without high school, this team was the only way for him to get seen by college and professional scouts. More importantly, it allowed him to continue being an athlete, despite the risk involved.

"I don't want to say it saved my life, but it brought me back to being an athlete," Larkin said. "I wasn't playing anymore in high school. That was fine, so I played summer ball."

Larkin played a key role for Midland and got looks from several Division I schools. Despite being drafted by Barry's Cincinnati Reds in the 40th round in 1991, he decided to play at the University of Texas. Despite knowing his medical history, the university stopped letting him play part way through his freshman year, due to the risk involved in him being on the field. Again, doctors warned he could die on the field if he continued to play.

Texas sat Larkin for about a week, then sent him to the National Institutes of Health in Bethesda, Maryland. Larkin, who hadn't dealt with many of the symptoms of hypertrophic cardiomyopathy since that morning his junior year of high school, was confident he was healthy enough to continue playing.

"I said, 'I feel great, I'm in great shape,'" Larkin said. "'There's no way I'm going to see this doctor and have him run me through all these tests and have him tell me I can't play. . . . I just didn't let it get me down. I said, 'Okay, I'll go. I'll take these tests. I'll pass them and then I'll come back and play ball.'"

Larkin was right. He was eventually cleared to keep playing. Around the time Larkin was cleared to play, his brother Barry continued to establish himself as one of the best players in the National League, being named to his fourth All-Star team and winning his fourth Silver Slugger at shortstop in 1991. With the national stage a program like Texas provided, Stephen thought he might be able to reach the big leagues like Barry one day.

After being cleared at Texas, Larkin continued his journey. It was one only made possible by his parents' belief in his dream. As they had encouraged Barry, Michael, and Byron before him, they had helped him confirm his decision to suit up, and thus to be seen by Texas in the first place.

"My parents grew athletes. My mom and dad sat me down and asked, 'Is this something you want to do?'" Larkin remembered. "Of course, I said, 'Mom, this is what we do.' She said, 'All right baby, if you want to play, we'll find you somewhere to play.' That was that."

In the subsequent two years of Stephen's collegiate career, his condition was a nonissue. He was able to go through rigorous workouts and seasons without showing any ill effects. He even played in two College World Series with the Longhorns.

"It never came up again," Larkin said. "I was just another one of the guys in the fall season getting ready for spring ball. That's just the way I wanted it."

Putting his condition out of his mind, Larkin was able to refocus on baseball. It's also worth noting that hypertrophic cardiomyopathy is a chronic disorder, so it can be lifelong or it can last several years before symptoms subside. Thus, by the end of his collegiate career, the possibility lurked in Larkin's mind that he was done dealing with this loathsome disorder.

After his junior year, Larkin was drafted by an MLB team for the second time. His decision to go to Texas had been a good one. Cincinnati had drafted him in the 40th round in 1991. After playing for three years with the Longhorns, he was drafted in the 10th round by the Texas Rangers in 1994.[4] Like his brother Barry, his collegiate career had driven his stock up, big-time. Again, the team he was playing for wanted to make sure he would be physically capable of contributing for them.

"When I got drafted, they sent me to a specialist in Dallas and again, I went through a battery of tests," Larkin said. "I went through a physical, a little more than the regular player that got drafted, but the guy said, 'You look good, you're fine. Go play. I hope to see you in the big leagues someday.'"

After being deemed physically proficient for elite-level competition, Larkin's professional baseball career began. After being drafted in June, he reported to the Rangers' Low-A affiliate, the Hudson Valley Renegades. Just a few weeks into his professional career, the infamous 1994 MLB players strike began. When it appeared MLB might have to use replacement players for the 1995 season, the Rangers' organization called all their minor-league players together.

"We had a meeting and our farm director said, 'Some guys are going to be asked to cross and go to the big leagues as replacement players. If you refuse, we're not going to hold it against you, but it would be good if you would go play,'" Larkin remembered. "Some guys were asked to go play; I was never asked. I think they knew not to ask me, with Barry being my brother, because I wouldn't have gone anyway."

Replacement players were never needed; the two sides came to an agreement before the 1995 season that brought major leaguers back by spring training. As he watched his brother Barry continue to dominate for the Reds, Stephen made strides of his own. Through the 1994 season, Barry had a career .296 batting average with 87 home runs, 188 steals, 1,164 hits, and a .360 on-base percentage to go along with six All-Star Game appearances, a Gold Glove, and five Silver Sluggers.

Stephen was optioned to the Charleston Riverdogs, the Rangers' A-ball affiliate, out of spring training. Through 113 games there, he was hitting .255 with 25 extra-base hits and eighteen steals. His Charleston, South Carolina, team took on the Charleston, West Virginia, team—the Cincinnati Reds–affiliated AlleyCats—in a weekend series late in the year. The two teams got into a bench-clearing brawl during the Friday game, bad blood boiling over between the two clubs.

Larkin arrived at the park the next day and was asked by manager Mike Berger to join him in his office.

"Lark, I have some good news, and I have some bad news," Larkin recalled Berger telling him. "The good news is: you've been traded."

"Oh okay, fun," Larkin thought to himself as Berger continued. The prospect of landing somewhere new excited him, and he pictured a fresh new squad with whom he might take the next major step in his career.

"The bad news is: you've been traded," Berger said. "You got traded to the Cincinnati Reds today and they want to send you to Charleston."

"Didn't we just fight those guys yesterday?" Larkin responded. Suddenly the picture of his fresh new baseball home had changed to something more foreboding.

Had Larkin reported directly to the AlleyCats like the Reds had initially wanted, he would have been on the other side of a heated rivalry that had resulted in a brawl the previous day. Instead, Berger sent Larkin back to his apartment to pack his truck and everything else up. He had him come back to the park and watch the game from the stands so they could figure out what they were going to do after the game. Instead of sending him to Charleston, the Reds opted to send him to Winston-Salem, North Carolina, to join the High-A Warthogs.

Larkin played 13 games for the Warthogs in 1995 as the season wound to a close. Soon after he was traded to the Reds organization, he watched Barry win the National League MVP Award. As he approached his own major-league dream, there was now a unique wrinkle to his ultimate goal.

"The first thing that hit my mind when I got the news I was traded was, 'I'm going to get to play in the big leagues with my brother,'" Larkin said. "That was the very first thought."

His goal was now not only to reach the big leagues, but to reach the big leagues so he could play on the same team as his older brother. It gave impetus beyond the inherent one of reaching the world's highest form of baseball competition.

"Just to have my mom and dad in the stands, watching their two sons playing in the same ballpark, on the same field, was motivation every day," Larkin said.

Stephen noted few differences between the way the Rangers and Reds were run as organizations. He split time in 1996 and 1997 between High-A Winston-Salem and the A-ball Charleston AlleyCats, the very team with which he'd brawled in 1995. He played in only 80 games in 1998, but was moving up, playing first base for the Double-A Chattanooga Lookouts.

Late in the 1998 season, Larkin was playing in Plant City, Florida, in the instructional league to get more game work before the offseason began. There were no games on Sundays in the instructional league. Larkin was confused, then, when he received a call from the Cincinnati Reds' farm director on a Sunday.

"He says, 'You need to get to the ballpark right now,'" Larkin recalled. "I was like, 'Uh oh. What did I do? Did I get released or something?'" If he had been playing that day, he likely would have been rapidly sending text messages to teammates, trying to find out if they, too, had received mysterious summons to the park.

Larkin arrived at the ballpark shortly after and was told to pack up his locker. Stephen was confused. He remembers fearing the worst.

"I was like, 'What?' I thought I got released and was thinking back like, 'Oh, lord, what did I do? Did I do something wrong?'" Larkin asked himself.

He went to his locker, grabbed his glove and spikes and put them in a bag, and returned to his coach's office. A hand extended out to shake Stephen's.

"Congratulations, you just got called up to the big leagues," he was told.

Stephen was driven to the airport then put on a plane back to his hometown of Cincinnati where he would join the Reds and his brother

Barry for the 1998 regular-season finale against the Pirates. He arrived at the ballpark the following day and was greeted by his many new teammates, who offered words of encouragement. If it was ever a mystery whether Stephen would get to play in the season finale, it didn't last long.

"I look up at the lineup card and I'm hitting third and playing first," Larkin said. "I thought, 'Holy shit.'"

After everyone became aware the youngest Larkin was starting that day, they stopped at his locker to give him a pat on the back for support. He was getting dressed at his locker, having a hard time calming his nerves before the game about which he'd dreamt his entire life. Current New York Yankees manager and then Reds third baseman Aaron Boone came up to Larkin with the intention of calming him down.

"Come with me, man," Larkin recalled Boone telling him as he took him to the batting cage to play soft toss. "He's like, 'Dude, calm down. Why are you so nervous? It's just another ball game.'"

That message clicked with Larkin, and he slowly began to settle down as the pair continued to get cuts in during soft toss.

"Once he said that, I'm like, 'You know what? It is just another ball game,'" Larkin said. "He said, 'Just get out there and do what you do, man.' I calmed down and just went out there and played."

He got onto the field and looked a few rows up the first-base line to see his parents, Robert and Shirley. They beamed with pride as they once again prepared to see one of their sons reach the pinnacle of his sport.

"The first thing I wanted to see when I went out there was my mom and dad in the stands," Larkin said. "That was the best part."

The jitters largely out of the way, Larkin was finally ready to take the field for his major-league debut. For the first time in their lives, Barry and Stephen were playing on the same baseball team. That competitiveness from the Larkins' backyard close to Cincinnati's Riverfront Stadium came out again before the Reds took their initial at bats in the home half of the first.

"We come out of the dugout and we're getting ready to go hit and Barry goes, 'Yo, man. Let's see who can hit the ball the hardest today.' Then he turns around and walks off," Stephen recalled. "I was like, 'Oh, okay, it's on.' . . . We'd been competitive and been athletes our whole life, so that wasn't any surprise to me. I was dead set on hitting the ball harder than he did that whole day."

He was batting third, behind Barry, who was batting second. While he was in the on-deck circle, preparing for his first career at bat, he was watching Barry in the batter's box. Also in the lineup that day were second baseman Bret Boone and third baseman Aaron Boone. The entire infield was made up of two pairs of brothers, the first and only time that has happened in MLB history.[5]

"I really didn't realize that until after the fact," Stephen said. "I had been in big-league camp, so looking around the infield seeing those guys wasn't really a big deal, because we had done it in spring training."

In Barry's first at bat, he grounded out meekly to third base. Stephen followed him, walking up to the box for his first at bat. He lined Jose Silva's first pitch to left field, but it was caught by Adrian Brown to end the inning.[6] In their first round of competition for the day, Stephen had hit the ball much harder but had no more to show for it than Barry.

Barry struck out swinging in his second at bat against Silva. Stephen followed suit by striking out swinging as well. In his third at bat, in the bottom of the sixth, Barry popped out to shortstop, giving Stephen a chance to gain the upper hand. Tied 1–1 and facing Silva for the third time, Larkin slapped the fifth pitch of the at bat through the hole between first and second base. It rolled into right field. He'd gotten his first career major-league hit.

"I rounded first base and came back to first. Our first-base coach tapped me on the butt and said, 'Good job brother, good swing.' He told me to look over to pick up my signs."

Larkin did exactly that, but then he was substituted for a pinch-runner, giving him a chance to take in the moment. It allowed the Reds crowd, who had fallen in love with his older brother for the past 12 seasons, to recognize his accomplishment too. He trotted back toward the dugout, again looking a few rows up the first-base line.

"On my way to the dugout, I looked up and wanted to make eye contact with my mom," Larkin said. "She's standing up clapping, and I just pointed at her, touched my heart, and told her, 'Thank you.' . . . It was the best day of my life."

Think about Robert and Shirley Larkin. Imagine the pair watching their two sons take the field together on the game's biggest stage. You might assume that it was among the best days of their lives as well.

He was able to appreciate the moment created by getting pinch-run for, but Larkin's competitive juices made him wish he had gotten to stay on the base paths. He could have jogged home on an Aaron Boone three-run homer a few batters later.

"I wanted to stay in the game, because I lined out my first at bat, struck out my second at bat and got the base hit in my third at bat," Larkin said. "I wanted to go 2-for-4, because he was coming up again."

Larkin was, of course, referring to his big brother, who, even in the last game of the regular season in which the Reds had no chance of making the playoffs, was staying in the game. He would get an extra plate appearance, giving him a chance to match or exceed Stephen's contributions at the plate that day. In the backyard, the brothers would have called that unfair, but that night at Riverfront, that was life.

Stephen got back to the dugout as everyone slapped him on the helmet and told him "good job." He sat down, grabbed a Gatorade and some sunflower seeds, and enjoyed the moment on the bench with Barry. He watched the rest of the game from the dugout.

Reds skipper Jack McKeon (25 years removed from managing Gary Martz in Kansas City) came up to Barry to ask him if he wanted one more at bat so the two brothers could have a chance at recording hits in the same game. As if it were ever a question, Barry came up for his fourth plate appearance to face hard-throwing Javier Martinez in the bottom of the eighth with the Reds leading 4–1.

A September call-up with something to prove, Martinez was touching triple digits with his fastball. On the third pitch of the at bat, he hit Larkin with one of those fastballs square in the ribs. Barry had a contusion that didn't go away for more than two months. When he got back to the dugout, he expressed his disappointment in not getting a chance to match Stephen's hit total.

"Man, I really wish I would've had that last at bat," Stephen remembered his older brother telling him in the dugout.

"I wish I had my last at bat too," Stephen jabbed back.

Then, for once letting the competition subside, Barry hugged his youngest brother and told him, "Good job, man. Congratulations."

"It was an all-day thing for me," Larkin said, looking back on his big-league debut. "In the clubhouse after I took a shower and sat down, I was able to realize what I had just done. . . . I always think about seeing my parents in the stands . . . seeing them standing up and clapping and smiling, just doing something to make them proud was the best thing for me."

Barry Larkin played in 2,180 regular-season games and 17 playoff games. He hit .353 in the 1990 World Series as the Reds swept the Athletics to win the championship. Still, when looking back on his 19-year career, September 27, 1998, sticks out.

"To this day, that final game of the 1998 season still stands out as one of the most special games I was ever a part of," Barry wrote in the *Players' Tribune*.[7]

Stephen was optioned to Double-A the following season and never got back to the big leagues. He held on to his dream for six more seasons, trying to make it back.

"Baseball has been in my blood since I was born," Larkin said. "I bounced around and played some independent ball, played overseas one summer, and just being an athlete and chasing that dream kept me going. . . . I never thought about it as not getting another chance. It just wasn't in the cards. It would have been great to be back in the big leagues, but I don't have any regrets. I just didn't make it."

In 2012, Barry Larkin was inducted into the National Baseball Hall of Fame. He brought Stephen along as a hitting instructor for a time when he got into coaching. Now, Stephen gives private hitting lessons in Cincinnati. In the summers, he coaches college players in a summer wood bat league, passing down his advice and experience to the next generation of players.

"I tell guys that pretty much every day I'm at the ballpark as a coach, I'm still learning something new," Larkin said. "Especially with baseball, you want to be a sponge. You might hear the same idea, but if you're in the cage with five different people, it's going to come out different for each one of them."

His playing career over, Larkin now has some new career goals. Ever the competitor, he wants to reach baseball's highest level as an instructor and coach.

"Just like it's every player's dream, now as a coach, I want to coach in the big leagues or at some professional level," Larkin said. One has to imagine that it would be much more difficult to *coach* in just one major-league game.

He's open to coaching in the minor leagues or overseas if that's where his career takes him. Another success story in a long line of Larkin athletic success stories, Stephen has more ahead of him. A fixture in Larkin's world his entire life now serves as an avenue by which he helps younger players who, like he once did, are chasing the dream of playing in the big leagues.

Stephen Larkin did so much to hold on to a game that was repeatedly almost torn from him. After spending his youth watching a road to athletic greatness being paved before him, he was forced to wonder if he would ever have the chance to walk it himself. His own heart, and the caution of the people who run the game, threatened his efforts to claim his piece of baseball greatness; but when you're a child of Robert and Shirley Larkin, you always have two hearts beating for you, with enough fortitude to propel you to the height of your potential.

Those many years ago, when Stephen was cycling through different stages of uncertainty, his mother had made him a promise: "We'll find you a place to play," she'd declared. And like that, as a devoted mother often can, she spoke a dream into existence. Stephen spent his whole life at home surrounded by coaches and teammates at the breakfast table before school. For him, to include and instruct today's youth in this game is to express love, as simply and as unconditionally as he has seen it expressed his whole life.

The love of his family, the sacredness of his health, and the relentless competitive spirit that defined his success were all symbolized by this one game; baseball was emblematic of a lifetime's worth of its most precious and satisfying of things. It's no wonder, then, that Larkin sees himself as owing so much to the sport.

"I just want to continue to give back to this game that has given me so much."

8

JON RATLIFF

September 15, 2000

Growing up in Syracuse, New York, Jon Ratliff played Little League like every other grade-school kid he knew. It slowly became apparent, though, that Ratliff was unlike most grade-school children when it came to throwing a baseball. Like so many of those children, Ratliff dreamed up his professional sports career before he was close to making it a reality.

"From the time I could play, I always had a dream of playing in the major leagues and thought that I was going to do that," Ratliff said. "I told anybody that would listen that it was what I was going to do."

By the time he was dominating older hitters as a sophomore in high school, he started to realize the major-league dream wasn't as lofty as it is for most kids wanting to throw a baseball to earn a paycheck. His all-star team had reached the Babe Ruth World Series, and he had been the team's star pitcher.

"I was a 16-year-old pitching against some of these 18-year-olds that were going to Georgia Tech and schools like that. That's when I started to know I could compete," Ratliff said.

If that didn't tip him off, being drafted in the 22nd round by the San Diego Padres in 1990 certainly affirmed he had the stuff to eventually crack the bigs. Ratliff didn't think he was ready for pro ball yet, though, so he turned the Padres down and went to college instead.

Despite being drafted out of high school, Ratliff had just one Division I college offer, from LeMoyne College, now a Division II program. In his first year at LeMoyne, Ratliff said, he led NCAA freshmen in ERA. It was in his sophomore year that he started to really open some eyes. He

Jon Ratliff warms up in the outfield at Oakland–Alameda County Coliseum before an Athletics game in 2001. *Courtesy of Jon Ratliff/Steve Fralick*

had a great regular season, which earned him a spot in the Cape Cod League, the revered college summer wood bat league.

"When I went to the Cape Cod League, that was the first time I really realized where I measured up and that I was pretty good," Ratliff said.

Pitching against guys he had seen play on TV in the College World Series from the likes of Florida State, Wichita State, and others, Ratliff realized a kid from upstate New York was as good as any of the players he was competing with or against. Scouts started to realize that too.

"[That fall], there were 20 or 30 scouts at every one of my games," Ratliff said.

Those scouts were first turned on to Ratliff by the fact that he made the Cape Cod All-Star team with flamethrower and future MLB star Billy Wagner. It was his great Cape Cod League season and All-Star selection that helped put him on the map.

"That's when I really started to realize, 'Okay, maybe I have a shot here,'" Ratliff said.

By the middle of his junior year at LeMoyne, it was evident Ratliff was going to be taken in the top two rounds of the MLB draft. With the pick they received as compensation for the Atlanta Braves signing Greg Maddux, the Chicago Cubs selected Ratliff with the 24th overall pick in the 1993 draft. [1]

Had the Cubs passed on him, Ratliff wouldn't have been on the board past pick 25. After being taken by Chicago, Ratliff's agent told him, "Well, if you didn't get picked by them, you were going to be the next pick by Oakland. Billy Beane loved you."

Instantly, the pressure was on. There wasn't just pressure in being a first-round pick, but in being a first-round pick from a college nobody had ever heard of, wondering what kind of talent he must have if he was taken so highly from a school with such a low national profile.

"With me, it was like, 'How the hell is this kid a first rounder?' I felt the pressure and you felt the eyes on you from the first time you were throwing in a bullpen in spring training, with everyone going, 'Well, who is this kid?'" Ratliff said.

Quickly, those expecting a lot out of Ratliff were out of Chicago. Just a couple of months into his professional career, the entire Cubs front office was blown up and a new staff was brought in. It completely changed Ratliff's outlook. The pressure he felt turned into a sense of urgency.

"The guys who stuck their neck out for me were no longer there," Ratliff said. "So, I felt like I better prove myself in a hurry, because I'm no longer a first-round pick, I'm just another number here trying to make it."

Despite the shake-up in the front office, Ratliff was moved quickly through the minor leagues. In his first professional season, he reached High-A ball. By the end of 1994, his first full professional season, he was a 22-year-old pitching in Triple-A.[2] The rapid call-ups helped his confidence, but it didn't necessarily help his development.

"Moving all over the place, I had four different pitching coaches that year [1994]," Ratliff said. "My pitching coach in Iowa would tell me one thing, my pitching coach in Daytona would tell me one thing, then I'd go to Orlando and he would tell me something else."

All the movement ultimately stunted Ratliff's growth, despite the fact he had worked himself to within one call of the big leagues before his 23rd birthday.

He was having trouble getting into a groove without the stability and consistency he needed to be at his best. "You're almost changing how you're throwing and what you're throwing on a weekly basis, because you have five different catchers who are calling different pitches and different sequences," Ratliff said.

His second full professional season, 1995, ended up being a pivotal one. It was one that would test his physical and mental makeup. Pitching the entire season for the Double-A Orlando Cubs, he went 10–5 with a 3.47 ERA. Cubs assistant general manager Larry Hines was at one of his Double-A starts, a dazzling gem.

"He came and watched me pitch and I threw a 68-pitch, complete game and had something like 21 ground-ball outs," Ratliff said.

"You could've pitched in the big leagues tonight," Ratliff remembered Hines telling him.

Hines continued, "There are five Randy Johnsons and there are five David Cones in the world. Then, there are 200 guys just like you. About 100 of them are in the big leagues and 100 of them are in the minor leagues. You have the ability to get there. The rest is up to you."

This clicked with Ratliff, someone who a year earlier had been watching big-league games, seeing if something would break his way to get him the call he'd always dreamed of.

"In my years in Triple-A, especially in my years with the Cubs, I'd be watching games on TV," Ratliff said. "I'd be watching WGN every afternoon, almost waiting for somebody to get hurt to see if you're getting the call. You always sort of knew you were there, but you were always in that one level below."

Ratliff felt like he was major-league ready but could sense the Cubs didn't feel the same way. That allowed doubt to creep into his mind, something he said he dealt with his entire career. It's something he said every prospective major leaguer has to deal with on their journey to or out of "The Show."

"You get into pro ball and it's 400 or 500 kids in the locker room and we're all fighting for X number of spots as you move your way up," Ratliff said. "I don't know that those doubts ever end. I had them my whole career."

After the 1995 season, Ratliff played in the Arizona Fall League as the top pitcher for his team in a league made up of baseball's top prospects. If there was any confusion why he may have doubted himself to that point, there was little confusion as he entered the locker room near the end of the fall league season.

"I still will never forget walking into the clubhouse and every single guy on my team was on a 40-man roster the day they came out," Ratliff said. "Everyone was on a roster except me. I was the lead pitcher on our team and we ended up winning the Arizona Fall League that year."

The Cubs' front office didn't show him the confidence they once had in him. By leaving him off the 40-man roster, they made him available in MLB's Rule 5 draft.

"Confidence-wise, that crushed me," Ratliff said. "That was the first year I had a really good year in Double-A, I had a really good year in the Arizona Fall League, and I thought I was on the right track for everything."

Ratliff, after not being placed on the Cubs' 40-man roster, had something to prove as the Arizona Fall League wound to a close. His manager, Bruce Kim, who was also his manager in Double-A with the Cubs, told him he would have taken Ratliff over two other guys who made the 40-man roster and that he should pitch with a vengeance in his last AFL start.

According to Ratliff, Kim told him, "Go out there. You have one start left. Go out there and show everyone why you belong on the 40-man and shove it up their ass."

He did. Ratliff had a great outing. Even so, it wasn't going to reverse a decision the Cubs' front office had already made.

"I went out and pitched six innings of one-hit baseball. I crushed it. I remember Bruce giving me a huge hug and he was happy for me," Ratliff said. "You need those guys; you need somebody to believe in you."

For as much as Kim believed in Ratliff, it didn't seem like the Cubs' front office believed in him anymore. His outing to close out the AFL season did little to change their minds.

"That still wasn't enough. It was just one game," Ratliff said. "The fact I won ten games in Double-A as a 23-year-old and then won four more games in the fall league with the best prospects in baseball, I was just flustered as to what I needed to do."

The Detroit Tigers gave him a chance to show what he could do, selecting him in the Rule 5 draft, taking him away from the Cubs. After putting together a solid spring, Ratliff's chance with a new organization came to an end. Like Chicago, Detroit did not put Ratliff on its 40-man roster to start the season, meaning he would return to the Cubs, per Rule 5 draft regulations.

After pitching two mediocre seasons with the Cubs, split between Double-A and Triple-A, Ratliff was buried on the organizational depth chart despite Chicago's struggles at the major-league level. Entering the 1998 season, Ratliff decided it was time for a change of scenery. He signed with the Atlanta Braves, the team whose compensatory pick had been used on him by the Cubs.

"We actually had a couple laughs when I went to the Braves and I went to a couple dinners with Maddux and we talked about it and we toasted the fact that, 'Hey, we showed the Cubs,'" Ratliff recalled. Maddux would, of course, return to the Cubs several seasons later, a bridge rebuilt between an organization and one of their best pitchers in generations.

Ratliff racked up 17 wins over the next two seasons with the Braves' Triple-A affiliate in Richmond. In each season, he was named the organization's top Triple-A pitcher.

"I spent two years in Triple-A with the Braves with horrible teams and was awarded Pitcher of the Year both years. I was given the award at Turner Field, for the best pitcher in Triple-A," Ratliff said. "Then, I'm watching guys in Double-A get the call over me."

The timing never seemed right for Ratliff, who believes he would have ended up pitching at Wrigley Field if he had put up similar numbers with the Cubs' organization in 1998 and 1999.

"Those two years, as well as I pitched, if I'm still on the Cubs, certainly I would have gotten to the big leagues for parts of a couple years," Ratliff said. "At the same time, you never know, because if someone doesn't believe in you, you're not going to get that shot."

Ratliff couldn't nail down what it was about him that failed to instill that sort of belief in the powers that be, and he couldn't figure out what others around him were doing right.

After those two seasons with the Braves, Ratliff received a phone call the minute he became a minor-league free agent.

"When I became a free agent, Billy Beane called my agent at three o'clock on the nose and he said, 'We've been trying to get you for years. Your timing was finally right,'" Ratliff remembered.

His timing could have been better. Looking back, Ratliff would have preferred to have slipped to the Athletics at no. 25 overall in the 1993 MLB draft.

"In Oakland, it was basically a train to the big leagues. They had some success and were building some good, young arms," Ratliff said. "I wish I had been the 25th pick instead of the 24th pick. I think things would have been totally different in my career."

Signing on with the Athletics for the 2000 season, Ratliff and the front office believed he'd be a good fit as someone who could potentially reach the major leagues quickly. It came down to timing again for Ratliff, as he saw a wave of young pitching talent in Oakland, which would soon garner national attention.

The framework for Ratliff's development with the Athletics was laid out in a meeting with Beane, who planned for him to be a major-league contributor.

"We think Jon can be a force for us. We have Tim Hudson, who won nine games last year as a rookie," Ratliff said he was told by Beane. "We'll see what happens the second time around the league with him. Then we have two young left-handers, Mark Mulder and Barry Zito, who are both probably a year away."

Mulder and Zito were closer to the big leagues than expected, and that hurt Ratliff's chances of becoming a major-league regular with Oakland.

"Zito won the Cy Young the next year. Mulder was in the big leagues two starts into that year," Ratliff said. "It was like I went from Atlanta East to Atlanta West. That's how I got lost in the shuffle there. . . . I still remember getting sent down in spring training after having a really good spring and [coach] Rick Peterson telling me, 'If you were with us five years ago, you would have been our no. 3 starter.' I thought, 'Oh, great. Now, I can be the no. 3 starter in [Triple-A] Sacramento.'"

Oakland's organizational depth allowed doubt to creep back into Ratliff's mind. He would constantly ask Triple-A manager Bob Geren if Billy Beane truly thought he could make it with the Athletics in the big leagues.

"I'd always ask Bob, 'Is Billy planning on calling me up and giving me a chance to pitch in the pen or does he just view me as an insurance policy in Triple-A?'"

Ratliff said Geren would consistently reassure him that Beane liked him and eventually wanted to see him get a shot at the major-league level.

Were it not for a groin injury, Ratliff would have gotten that shot in July 2000.

"They needed a spot starter in Colorado for a doubleheader. I missed a start for a groin pull and it happened to be right then," Ratliff said. "I was the obvious choice to get that start and they ended up giving it to another guy who had come up from A-ball at the beginning of the year and was basically just an organizational guy. . . . He ended up getting the start in Colorado. It seemed like, once again, my timing sucked."

Shortly after being passed on for the spot start against the Rockies, Ratliff's timing finally matched up with the timing of the organization he was with. He got called into manager Bob Geren's office. He thought he was going to be scolded. He was wrong.

"He starts going off about how he's tired of the injuries and how he's not going to put me out there if I'm not healthy and then he basically had our pitching coach, Rick Rodriguez, go over the opposing lineup," Ratliff said.

Rodriguez started rattling off the lineup: "Leading off, we have Bernie Williams. Hitting second, we have Derek Jeter."

Suddenly, Ratliff realized what was going on, and he couldn't contain himself any longer.

"At that point, I had tears in my eyes and was like, 'You have to be kidding me,'" Ratliff said. "I went up and I was in Oakland the next day.

It was the end of August and we were playing against the Yankees in front of 45,000 people the next day." Finally, it seemed like his timing had lined up. That wasn't quite the case, however.

Ratliff got to take in the excitement of being in a major-league atmosphere, but nearly a week passed and he hadn't pitched. The team needed a third catcher in the midst of a playoff push. A. J. Hinch, eventual manager of the 2017 World Series champion Houston Astros, was called up and Ratliff was optioned back down.

"As thrilling as it was to go to the big leagues, I waited seven years to do it, got there, was there for five days and didn't pitch," Ratliff said.

Upon returning to Triple-A, Ratliff was shaken up. Geren told him he looked miserable, and Ratliff told him it was because he had been called up, didn't pitch, and had no guarantee of ever getting back to the big leagues again. Geren assured him he would be back.

He turned out to be right. Ratliff was called up again in September after the minor-league playoffs had concluded. He knew this meant he would be with Oakland for the remainder of the regular season.

"I got at least three weeks there where I'm going to be putting on a big-league uniform in a big-league stadium and enjoying a pennant race and all that," Ratliff said. "What a better time to be there. I think it validated everything that I had worked for."

With all that time, even in the middle of a division race, Ratliff felt confident he would finally get into a game. On September 15 against the Tampa Bay Devil Rays, the Athletics offense helped him out. With Barry Zito pitching, they scored 13 runs in the first five innings, giving the A's an 11-run lead.[3] As Zito's pitch count climbed, it became apparent that Ratliff's major-league debut would likely come at Tampa Bay's Tropicana Field.

"Everyone from the sixth inning on, like Jason Isringhausen would walk by me and would pull on my jersey acting like my heart was coming out of my chest, like, 'You're going to get in today, you're going to get in,'" Ratliff said. "So, when I knew it was going to be my debut, it built to that."

His dreams became a reality when a call was placed from the Oakland dugout to the bullpen.

"Once they called down, the adrenaline started pumping," Ratliff said.

He was going to get the ninth inning in a 17–3 game.

"I jogged to the line slowly and took in my surroundings as I was walking toward the field," Ratliff said.

"Keep us moving here, young fella," Ratliff remembered third-base umpire Jeff Kellogg telling him.

Ratliff, still able to vividly recall his debut, remembers just about every pitch he threw. He only threw 12.

"The first pitch was strike one and then I threw a really good slider the guy swung and missed on and I'm like, 'All right, this is it,'" Ratliff said. "Then I got a little rollover ground ball to third base and Mark Bellhorn, who was my third baseman all year in Sacramento, was the guy fielding the ball. They throw it around the horn and he gives me a little wink and I'm like, 'All right, that's one out in the big leagues in the books.'"

Ratliff looked over to the Devil Rays' dugout. He saw pitching coach Bill Fischer, who was his pitching coach with the Richmond Braves. Fischer was someone who had always told him he'd be able to pitch at Turner Field with the Braves. Although he hadn't been able to see that prophecy through, Ratliff appreciated having a token of his invisible battle present for the moment it all had been for.

"It was nice that a guy who believed in me for that long got to see it come to fruition," Ratliff said.

His former coach looked on as his Devil Rays tried to muster some offense. They couldn't. Ratliff was locked in for the five minutes he was on the mound. The second batter of the inning, Gerald Williams, meekly popped out to first base for the second out. On the 12th pitch of Ratliff's day, he got Toby Hall to fly out to center field. He had pitched a perfect inning in the big leagues.

"It was one-two-three really quickly. Although the 12 pitches should be really quick, I remember after the game, just being wiped out from all the adrenaline from my one inning," Ratliff said, "but I had a big smile on my face and I took that back with me to the hotel."

Ratliff had thought ahead and made sure his memory wouldn't be the only place his major-league debut would last.

"Luckily, I had a buddy of mine from college have a tape ready anytime I came in," Ratliff said. "So, if I was warming up in the bullpen, he would try to tape the debut, and I ended up getting a tape from him of that inning. . . . I've replayed it obviously, and shown my kids. It didn't seem as quick when I watch now on TV as it seemed when I was pitching, but it definitely went quickly."

There were two other games in which Ratliff came very close to pitching. With the team in Oakland, taking on the Angels on September 28, Ratliff got loose as the game moved deep into extra innings. He continued to throw and was told the 15th inning would be his.[4] The only problem is that he was told that before the bottom of the 14th. As he kept throwing in the bullpen, Troy Glaus smacked a three-run walk-off homer, ending the game and Ratliff's hopes of appearing in it.

"When we went 14 innings against the Angels and they literally point to me and say, 'You've got next inning,' and boom they hit a home run and the game is over, it's like, 'Oh, my god,'" Ratliff said.

The team also had Ratliff throw bullpens in the final days of the season, because he was going to make a spot start on the final day of the year if the A's had already clinched the AL West title. The final game of the season ended up mattering, with the Athletics needing to win in order to go to the playoffs.

On October 1, the Athletics beat the Rangers 3–0 and surprised everybody by winning the American League West with one of the youngest cores in baseball: Mulder, Zito, Miguel Tejada, and Eric Chavez had all yet to turn 25.

"We all picked [Jason] Giambi up on our shoulders and walked him off the field," Ratliff said. "There were about 50,000 people in the Coliseum. Everybody in the crowd is chanting 'M-V-P!,' which Jason wound up winning. It was just unbelievable."

In addition to his one appearance on the mound, winning the division on the final day of the regular season remains one of Ratliff's career highlights. For as poor as the timing of his career was as a whole, he got to experience winning a division title with a team on the cusp of a great four-year stretch.

"The way it all happened was like a storybook ending, which is pretty awesome," Ratliff said. "I still remember standing next to Billy Beane and Art Howe and thanking them for letting me be a part of it."

Ratliff played in just 22 games in 2001, mostly in Triple-A, before an elbow injury forced him into surgery. He missed the rest of 2001 and the start of the 2002 season. Less than a year and a half after competing for a major-league roster sport, Ratliff felt buried on the Athletics' organizational depth chart, just as he had been with the Cubs earlier in his career.

"I'm going to spring training with the A's and battling for the fifth starter spot and here I am, 15 to 16 months later and I'm mopping up in front of 500 people in some Triple-A stadium," Ratliff said. "I told my-self when I was doing really well in 1999 and 2000 that if I ever got the feeling that I couldn't get back to the big leagues or I wasn't going to get back to the big leagues, what am I playing for? I played eight years of Triple-A; I don't need to keep doing this."

Retirement was already on Ratliff's mind going into the 2002 offsea-son. The writing was on the wall: his time competing for the major leagues was over.

"I remember Dick Scott, our minor-league director, coming around the last week of the season and talking to guys," Ratliff said. "He goes, 'You threw the ball really well coming off of surgery, the stuff is coming back.' . . . Then he said, 'Have you ever thought about coaching?'"

Ratliff knew then that it was time for him to give up the game he loved. He called his agent and told him his decision.

"I'm like, 'You know what? I think I'm done. I gave it my shot, but my arm wasn't feeling as good as I was hoping for after surgery,'" Ratliff recalled telling his agent.

Despite the arduous grind of the minor leagues, Ratliff's major-league dream had become a reality for mere minutes on a September day in Tampa. He was at peace with the fact that that would be his only major-league appearance.

"I felt like at that point, my career had run its course; I played ten years and played eight years in Triple-A," Ratliff said. "I got to the big leagues, I played for a division-winning team. I got my inning and I felt like after eight years of working for that one inning, I didn't have eight years left in me to work for another one."

Without that one inning, Ratliff may have tried even harder to get to the big leagues for just one taste of life in "The Show." After getting there and experiencing it, though, his decision was made easier. He wasn't working toward something he had never experienced before. His career felt more complete thanks to the spotless inning he threw in an Oakland A's uniform.

"I would have had a much harder time walking away after I was hurt if I had never gotten that one inning in the big leagues," Ratliff said. "But getting that one inning in the big leagues and actually getting called up made it, in some ways, easier to walk away than it would have been had I never gotten that shot."

Ratliff transitioned out of the game as his family began to grow. His three children, all athletes in their own right, know all about his story, but it's hard for Ratliff to properly explain the struggle and all that he still thinks about when it comes to his major-league career.

"I pitched in one game. I got three guys out. Nobody hit the ball out of the infield and I never got a shot to go out there again," Ratliff said. "I wish I could have a beer with one of the GMs that didn't call me up or give me a shot and take a look at the scouting report from my good years between 1997 and 2000. . . . I would love to see what the knock was on me, why I never did get that shot."

This is the sort of curiosity better left unsatisfied; if it's true what Larry Hines had told him during his days with Chicago, that he was merely one of 200 players, half of whom were cut out for the major leagues, then the thing keeping him from that shot was likely so arbitrary that knowing it would serve only to frustrate him further.

That's a torturous detail in the lives of these one-game players: in the course of an individual's life, some of the most significant events are often seemingly determined by the most minimal and inconsequential of factors.

With an extended shot, Ratliff is almost sure he could have had at least mild success in the MLB based on others he saw pass him on their way to the big leagues.

"The one regret I have from my entire career is I never got a shot to get five or six starts in the big leagues, I never got a shot to get ten relief appearances," Ratliff said. "I played with a lot of guys who I felt I was better than, or at least as good as, and some of them ended up with five-year major-league careers. . . . Once you get your two or three years in and show you're serviceable and you get outs, you tend to stay."

Ratliff never got a serious chance at sustainability. When you get such a small taste of something you've worked your whole life for, it's hard not to think back to it every now and then.

"I definitely drift back sometimes. You think about it whether you're just reminiscing a memory, posting something to Facebook, or seeing some of your other buddies post something to Facebook," Ratliff said.

All that drifting back has only pushed Ratliff forward in his postbaseball life. He now sells orthopedic implants, something that helps pitchers as well as position players deal with injuries. When being interviewed for his first job in the industry, he drew on his experience in baseball.

"The manager considering hiring me asked me, 'Well, can you handle rejection?' and I'm like, 'Yeah, I've been booed in front of 40,000 people and been written about in the paper the next day. I'm pretty sure I can handle going into an office and having a guy tell me he doesn't want to buy what I'm selling,'" Ratliff said.

His outward confidence developed from the thick skin necessary to sustain even the shortest of professional baseball careers. It's something minor leaguers tend to develop over time, as they deal with the ups and downs of life on the fringe of a big-league career.

"That was my career for ten years and the livelihood of going into a clubhouse in spring training and realizing that if there are 30 pitchers in camp, 11 to 12 of them are making the big-league roster, 11 to 12 of them are making the Triple-A roster, and the rest better go get another job or your career could be over," Ratliff said.

Using the psychological lessons he learned in a career riddled with poor timing and unanswered questions, Ratliff now works to get athletes the equipment necessary to deal with common injuries. When Mike Trout tore a ligament in his thumb in 2017, Ratliff says the brace he wore on his thumb was developed by his company.

Ratliff is now back in New York, where it all began. Out of the bubble of upstate New York, he burst onto the national scene, earning himself a shot at the big leagues.

He can always think back to September 15, 2000, where for a few minutes, he was the pitcher for the Oakland Athletics, in a game they won on their way to a division title.

9

RON WRIGHT

April 14, 2002

By the time he was a sophomore slugger at Kamiakin High School in Kennewick, Washington, power hitter Ron Wright realized he was ahead of the curve. Called up to varsity in the middle of his second high school season, he was coming into his own.

"It [playing varsity as a sophomore] didn't really happen much, because it was a big school. We had 2,200 students," Wright said.

It didn't exactly endear him to the varsity teammates whose playing time he was taking, but it did endear him to the scouts who seemed to keep showing up to his games in growing numbers. By the offseason before his senior year, those scouts had let him know he would have a chance to play in the big leagues at some point.

"Before my senior year, there were a few scouts who told me I was probably going to go in the top ten rounds."

As he dominated high school ball, Wright was just starting to grow into what would eventually become a 6'1", 230-pound frame. He was the star of the Kamiakin Braves by senior year.

The scouts knew what they were talking about. Wright went from one Braves team to another. He was taken in the seventh round of the 1994 MLB draft by the Atlanta Braves, a team he had grown up rooting for all the way from Washington.[1]

"In those times, you could only get one of two teams [on TV]: the Braves or the Cubs. I idolized Dale Murphy and the kind of person he was."

After deciding to root for the Braves, because he could watch them on TV, Wright was now a member of the organization. Quickly, though, he realized baseball is a business, and any rooting interest he had previously went away soon after he was drafted.

Wright entered the league as a fan of the team that drafted him. As his professional career got its official start, fans of teams around the country faced something they had long feared: a players' strike. It took place just months after Wright was drafted, putting him in a precarious position right off the bat. He saw it as temporary, though, and not something that would affect his long-term prospects in the league.

"I was like anybody else, thinking, 'These guys are getting paid so much,' but then on the other side of it, I started being in players' meetings and knowing what the owners were making," Wright said. "That made me see both sides of it and in the end, I ended up sticking up more for the players."

Wright opened his professional career with the Gulf Coast League Braves in 1994 and struggled, hitting just .172 in 179 plate appearances, hitting just one home run. By the time the dust settled and replacement players were leaving the game prior to the 1995 season, though, Wright started to figure out how to be a professional hitter.

He played the entire 1995 season for the Single-A Macon Braves. In his first full season of professional baseball, he hit .271 with 32 home runs and 104 RBIs. Equally important, he slugged 23 doubles and ended the season with an impressive .849 OPS. Atlanta's front office took notice, and he was invited to big-league spring training the following year.

"I was playing against guys that literally two years before, I had seen on TV. They were back in Triple-A kicking it around. It was weird to be idolizing them at 18 and a year later be in big-league camp with a locker next to them," Wright said.

"Johnson, McGriff, Glavine, Maddux—when I was drafted, those were the guys I was watching on TV. I started that first season in Macon and that next year, they invited me to camp and my locker was right there with them."

Wright was working his way up in professional baseball, and after his monster 1995 campaign, he looked to be on the fast track. Then, at just 20

Ron Wright cracks a smile while wielding a bat for the Calgary Cannons of the Pacific Coast League in 1997. *Courtesy of Ron Wright*

years old, he was blindsided by an aspect of baseball as a business: the team that had drafted him traded him away.

The power hitter was traded to the Pirates in the trade that brought Denny Neagle to Atlanta.[2] At the time of the trade, Neagle had 29 professional wins and was coming off a breakout 1995 season, which saw him make the National League All-Star team. While a trade often shatters a young player's confidence, it actually strengthened Wright's.

"It wasn't bitter, it was mostly sweet. I looked at it as a positive," Wright said. "I looked at it as an opportunity."

Being traded for an established major-league player marked a big step in Wright's journey to reach the big leagues, and he gave the Pirates' front office no reason to doubt their decision. In 1996, split between High-A ball and Double-A with the Braves and Double-A with the Pirates, Wright put up some gaudy numbers. By the time he was done demoralizing opposing pitchers, Wright had hit 36 bombs, driven in 114 runs, and registered a .908 OPS.

He was becoming a real offensive force, totaling 68 home runs and 218 RBIs in his first two full seasons in professional baseball. It was no surprise, then, when he was named baseball's no. 48 overall prospect by *Baseball America* going into the 1997 season. After getting his average up to .304 in 91 games in 1997, Wright was a September call-up for the Pirates. However, they made it clear they didn't want him to actually get in a game: Wright had had a wrist injury. The team was worried a check swing might cause long-term damage to the wrist.

The Pirates had told Wright he was going to be there for the next 10 to 12 years, so there was no need to rush back from injury. "We were going to take another month off and go down to the fall league," Wright remembers. "[The Pirates told me] we'll get you here either early next year or the start of the year and you'll be here for years and years."

Similar promises are often made in the periphery of the major leagues, and they are often made in times of extreme optimism. However, there is a reason why players who establish sustained careers within an organization are so highly regarded: there are innumerable factors along the way that can send a promise into the wind.

Pittsburgh had told Wright that within a month he would be up with their big-league club one way or another in 1998. The wrist became the least of Wright's health problems. During the 1997 fall league season, his back was bothering him. When he came to spring training the following year, the back pain hadn't gone away.

"I wasn't hitting for a very good average or able to adjust to things in the offseason," Wright said.

In a seemingly insignificant moment that spring, his career changed on a dime.

"I just went down to do the stretch where you go down to touch your toes and just felt a pop and I just crashed," Wright said. "It was the weirdest thing. My legs were just gone. I was pretty much numb from the waist down at that point."

Wright was taken to a hospital near the stadium and was then flown to Los Angeles. It was there he would have a disk surgically removed from his back.

As painful as the back injury was, Wright, now 22 and on the cusp of cracking the big leagues for good, thought it would be just a minor setback. It set off a course of events that would define Wright's professional career.

"I was still young and I got supposedly the best surgeon in the country. I didn't think I'd sit out the whole year. I thought we'd go get the surgery, do rehab for a little bit, but it didn't get better."

In order to improve his recovery, the surgical team decided to put him under again to clean up some of what they had done in the previous surgery. A mistake made in this surgery changed Wright's career goal of wanting to be a perennial all-star into an impossibility. Now, he hoped simply to just reach the big leagues.

"I was essentially hitting without a right leg and I was competing with guys that were on steroids for the rest of my career," Wright said.

During the surgery, doctors accidentally clipped Wright's sciatic nerve.

"The minute my nerve was cut, I was done."

The sciatic nerve runs from the lower back to the tips of the toes. It is the body's largest nerve. It enables movement and feeling to the thigh, knee, calf, ankle, foot, and toes.[3] When Wright's nerve was clipped, it took away the power from his right leg, the leg from which a right-handed hitter generates all of his power.

"When I woke up, my right leg was numb and he told me it would go away when the swelling goes down, but three weeks later, it was still numb," Wright said. "I go to spring training the next year and it doesn't really hurt, but it's not as strong as my left leg."

The numbness in Wright's right leg caused a series of other issues. Based on the severity of the injury, Wright's awareness of where his right leg was in relation to space was greatly diminished. A right-handed hitter drives with his back leg, starting with the hips, down to the hamstring, calf, ankle, and foot itself. With all of these areas affected by the damage to his sciatic nerve, Wright was unable to generate the raw power he was able to in the two seasons prior.

He had to turn to the mental side of the game that often separates the great hitters from the good ones.

"It's so narrow. People don't realize how narrow the competition is, especially mentally. I could hit it, I had good hands and good eyes and so I was able to put together some respectable years," Wright said.

Behind the eight ball or not, Wright now had to deal with trying to get back to the major leagues, something he was supposedly a month away from at the time of his sudden back injury during spring training.

By this time, Wright wasn't just battling his own body to get to the major-league level, he was battling others whose bodies were being enhanced by the use of steroids, a rampant problem in baseball by the late 1990s.

"I could hit 30 to 35 home runs. That was my strength, that is what upgraded me, but with steroids, you have second basemen and shortstops hitting that many home runs," Wright said. "So, the one thing you do better than anybody else is now a level field. Thirty home runs was nothing anymore. . . . By the time I retired, a clubhouse would look like a WWE locker room."

Although other players' steroid use put him at a disadvantage, Wright does not share the popular blanket view on juicers. Yes, they were cheaters, but Wright said people in many other professions would take advantage of something similar if given the opportunity to improve the craft they had dedicated their lives to.

"It isn't as simple as 'they're a cheater.' I still lost a lot of respect for the guys that did it, but it's not that clear cut," Wright said. "I saw guys that I still have respect for using them. I don't think they should have done it, but I totally get why they would."

Young competitors might choose to use steroids in order to shorten rehab time for an injury, to bring up their bat speed a few tenths of a second, or to be able to handle the rigors of major-league training and game schedules. All of these small advantages can establish the margin between a player who is afforded a real major-league opportunity and one who is not. Some of these benefits surely would have benefited Wright in his pursuit of major-league success. These factors don't justify the transgressions, but they do contextualize the decision made by an increasing number of young players during this time.

After playing in just 20 games between rookie ball and Triple-A in 1998, Ron Wright, the 6'1" righty, would get his first chance to show the Pirates he should still be in their plans 10–12 years down the road.

In 1999, Wright played in just 24 games, hitting .213 with zero home runs and four RBIs. His career, prepared for liftoff a year prior, was now in danger of never getting off the ground. However, in the following two years, he put together seasons that were impressive for a power hitter who wasn't able to drive off his back leg.

The 2000 season saw Wright hit .253 with an .824 OPS, 14 home runs, and 63 RBIs combined across Double-A and Triple-A in the Cincinnati Reds' farm system. Life in professional baseball can be brutal, though, as he changed organizations yet again in 2001, ending up in the Tampa Bay Devil Rays' system.

Spending the entire season playing for the Durham Bulls, Tampa's Triple-A affiliate, Wright took another step in the right direction, as he hit .262, slugged .800, and added 20 bombs while driving in 75 runs.

"I feel like I overachieved. I feel like I had better seasons than I probably should have. I felt like I got back to that level, which I felt fortunate enough to do. So, I just feel lucky," Wright said.

Despite having the rug pulled out from under him and his major-league dream, it is Wright's optimism that kept pushing him. After two solid seasons, mostly at the Triple-A level, the Seattle Mariners, the MLB team closest to where he went to high school in Washington, decided to bring him in as their everyday first baseman at Triple-A Tacoma.

Just two weeks into the season, Wright got the call he had always expected in the mid-1990s. By the early 2000s, it wasn't a call he was sure he would ever get.

"It was just exhilaration."

Perennial all-star and potential Hall of Famer Edgar Martinez ruptured his hamstring running out a ground ball to third in the ninth inning of an 8–4 win over the Texas Rangers. After an MRI revealed the severity of the injury, he was placed on the disabled list. Wright would be the man to take his spot on the 25-man roster while Martinez worked his way back from injury.

Wright was told to be on the next plane out to Dallas to join the Mariners, who were still in the middle of their series against the Rangers.

"Before the injury [clipped sciatic nerve], I don't think I would have been happy with anything less than an all-star career," Wright said. "But my number one goal was to play in the big leagues. At that point, it was just a huge weight off my shoulders. . . . It would have been tough to go all those years and have all that happen and not even get a taste."

The first people he told the good news to, naturally, were his parents. However, Wright told his parents to wait to come see him play. There would be time for them to catch him in a big-league game in either Seattle or New York, Wright told his folks. Wright is lucky his advice fell on deaf ears.

"They came out anyway. They didn't listen to me," Wright said. "My dad was a Yankees fan growing up and we were going to New York, so at that point, Edgar was down for 10 to 15 days and I figured they could see me play somewhere else."

"My dad said, 'Yeah, whatever,' hung up the phone and got a ticket."

Wright had to wait a few days to get his shot. Strange circumstances had shaped Wright's career to that point, and it was once again strange circumstances under which he'd get his first major-league opportunity.

The dream finally came true in Arlington, Texas, on April 14, 2002, at the expense of infielder Jeff Cirillo's face. Seattle was visiting Texas for the third game of a four-game set. Wright, once again, was not in the Mariners' starting lineup.

During batting practice, Mike Cameron hit a line drive that deflected off the pitching screen and hit Cirillo in the face. The injury required stitches and knocked him out of the lineup.

Quickly, Wright realized April 14, 2002, was a day he would always remember: the day of his MLB debut.

"I just remember thinking, 'Okay, Cirillo got hurt and they need someone in there.' In the middle of the daily grind, it was just like, 'Sweet, I get in there, but I hope he's okay.'"

Wright's career of seemingly random triumphs and pitfalls would be encapsulated by his MLB debut. Cirillo's pregame injury was far from the strangest thing that would happen in Arlington that afternoon.

Kenny Rogers, a legend by 2002 who had thrown a perfect game in 1994, was the opposing pitcher for Texas. Nearly 33,000 people were in attendance at the Ballpark at Arlington to witness what would turn out to be a historic day, even if it was lost to the annals of baseball history shortly thereafter.

It was windy, 76 degrees, and overcast on the mid-April afternoon. Derryl Cousins was the home-plate umpire. Marty Foster, Andy Fletcher, and Joe Brinkman were the umpires on the bases. Wright batted seventh behind two-time All-Star John Olerud. By the time the top of the second inning rolled around, the Mariners were already up 1–0 and threatening again.[4]

Wright strolled up to the plate for the first major-league plate appearance of his career. Runners were on first and second, nobody out.

The first pitch: 84-mile-per-hour fastball over the heart of the plate. Wright watched it go by.

"That's my only regret," Wright told the *New York Times*. "I should have swung at that first pitch."[5]

The at bat ended with Rogers striking Wright out, officially welcoming him to the big leagues.

The Mariners' threat was over when the next two batters failed to drive in Olerud or Ruben Sierra, the runners on first and second, respectively.

"Looking back on what happened in the actual game, it always felt kind of weird, like, 'Why would all that go down?' It's just weird. The whole thing is weird," Wright said, thinking back on the moment more than a decade and a half in the past.

Wright was referring to his next two at bats, which, in the lightest sense, made his only major-league game among the most memorable in MLB history.

Still up 1–0, the Mariners came to bat in the top of the fourth inning. Sierra led off the inning with a double. Olerud followed that up with a single, and Sierra was held at third. Wright was coming up with two runners on base yet again, and nobody out.

With a 2–2 count, Wright figured Rogers might come right at him. In the first ball he put in play in his major-league career, he grounded back to Rogers on the mound. Rogers turned and threw to shortstop Alex Rodriguez for the first out. Sierra was late breaking to the plate, and A-Rod fired home to catcher Bill Haselman, who threw back to third baseman Hank Blalock, who tagged Sierra out. Two outs had been made on the play, and it wasn't over yet.

Amid the chaos, Wright was waved around first and on his way to second. Blalock turned and threw to Rogers covering second base. Wright, like Sierra seconds earlier, was caught in a rundown. Rogers threw to second baseman Michael Young, covering first base, who tagged Wright out. In Wright's second career at bat, he had grounded into one of the strangest triple plays in the history of America's pastime.

According to the Society for American Baseball Research, in the 141-year history of Organized Baseball, this is the only time anyone has ever hit into a 1-6-2-5-1-4 triple play. It would be entirely unsurprising if we don't get another one in the next 141 years.

Through two at bats, Wright was now responsible for four outs and had stranded four runners on base. Of course, his second at bat really should have been an RBI fielder's choice, but a gaffe by Sierra had cost him that tally on the stat sheet.

"It really was a baserunning error as much as anything," Wright said. "If Ruben runs hard, maybe he scores and I get an RBI. Kenny was off balance when he fielded the ground ball. He goes to second, I figure I'll get an RBI, fielder's choice, but that's just baseball."

At bat no. 3 came with, yet again, two runners on and nobody out. Olerud and Sierra were once again on first and second for Wright to try and knock them in. With Rogers still in the game in the sixth inning, Wright swung at his first offering, trying not to let another hittable first pitch go by.

He drove the ball, but right at A-Rod, who initiated a more traditional 6-4-3 double play. Unbelievably, Wright had been accountable for six outs in just three at bats. Unsurprisingly, of the nearly 1,000 players to play just one game in the major leagues, no hitter has been accountable for more outs.

Wright recalled to the *New York Times* that the following day in Texas, a game in which he was not starting, manager Lou Piniella walked over to him in the dugout when Seattle put runners on first and second and jokingly said, "I'd put you in, but I'm afraid you'd hit into a triple play."[6]

Wright sees his first and only major-league game as a microcosm of his career as a whole.

"I played a lot of baseball at a really high level, but yeah, it was a bunch of weird things stopping it from reaching its potential," Wright said. "There was a lot of stuff out of my control that dictated how it went."

The tall, strong power hitter, who had gotten his first major-league call-up in 1997 with the Pirates, was removed from the game in the seventh inning for a pinch-hitter. With that, his MLB career came to an end. Some say all you leave on a baseball field are footprints and memories, but Wright got something a little better after the game: an exciting 9–7 Mariners win.

Teammate Bret Boone, who played a part in Stephen Larkin's only game, gave Wright the lineup card from that day signed by everyone on the Mariners and a few players on the Rangers.

"I look back now and it's sweet, because A-Rod signed it. All the guys on my team signed it. . . . Kenny Rogers signed it. I'm sure he was happy to," Wright said with a smile.

Wright keeps that scorecard in his briefcase to this day. His jersey from his one start in the big leagues gets a more prominent placement.

"I framed my jersey, because that meant a lot to me as a symbol of getting to actually play in the big leagues."

He has never seen a video of his lone major-league game. He says he was there and that's enough for him. Some of his friends don't even know he played in the big leagues.

"I don't talk about it a ton, but it was probably the hardest and most rewarding thing I'll ever do." Those two things often seem to be one and the same.

Through injury, through adversity, Wright did manage to get to the bigs. He played in just one major-league game, but it was his personal journey that gave him the perspective to appreciate his brief time at baseball's highest level.

"Before if you told me as a 21-year-old, hitting .300 and making the All-Star Game in Triple-A, 'You're going to play in one big-league game and you're going to go 0-for-3 and have that be your result,' I would have been devastated," Wright said.

But knowing what he did about his body and his injury, Wright realized that playing without registering a hit was much better than never getting into a game at all, a possibility that seemed increasingly likely as he battled through his sciatic nerve injury in the late 1990s through the early 2000s.

"Of course I'd love to have it be 1-for-3, but what does that really mean?" Wright said. "Maybe I have a decent month, but I know that wouldn't have been the case over the long run, because I just wasn't physically able to do it."

Wright was sent back down to Triple-A Tacoma a couple of days after his debut. His time in the majors was over, and he could sense it. He never allowed himself to believe his time in the big leagues could be up in the moment, but in hindsight, he realized that may have been his only shot at the major-league level.

He finished out that year putting up decent numbers in Triple-A, batting .273 with 15 homers and 57 RBIs to go along with an .810 OPS. Those numbers weren't enough for him to stick with the Mariners. He signed with the Indians and was assigned to the Double-A Akron Aeros. He ended up with the Tigers by season's end, playing for their Triple-A affiliate, the Toledo Mud Hens.

Following the 2003 season, Wright played one more year of professional baseball in the independent league with the Sioux Falls Canaries, but there was a growing sense within himself it might soon be time to hang up the spikes.

"As much as I love baseball, and loved baseball at the time, it was never more important than my family," Wright said.

Wright had a growing family and a supportive wife to think about, and after 28 games with Sioux Falls, he called it quits. Really, though, Wright never "quit," even at times when others may have given up.

His support system helped ease the pain of walking away from the game, but leaving the sport he had loved and poured his heart into still wasn't easy.

"Walking away is the toughest thing I ever did," Wright said. "But I've never thought 'poor me' outside of a couple times. Don't get me wrong; I'm human and it was hard to watch guys I was as good as go on and do really well, but at the same time, I was really happy for them. More than anything, you wonder: why?"

He handled the mental side better than most, likely because of his strong family support system and the fact he realized there was life beyond baseball. For some, with baseball being all they've ever known, it's hard to come to that realization and face it. That makes the transition and adjustment to life after the game a painful experience.

"If that's all you have to live for and you base all your success on the money you've made or whatever else in the game, what numbers you've achieved, I suppose if you don't have any of that [support system] and then you lose baseball, I can see why people would get very down," Wright said.

It's the game itself, though, that taught Wright more about himself than he could have ever learned on his own. It set him up for success in his life beyond the sport.

"I think sports are the last great place where you can learn about yourself and fail, especially at a high level."

With this in mind, Wright embarked on pursuing a career as a pharmacist. Compared to the internal and external pressures of baseball, this typically difficult path didn't seem too daunting to the newly retired ballplayer.

"[In baseball] you have to produce or the city hates you," Wright said. "It was a different career that was just an honor to be around for 10 years. After that, I didn't freak out over a pharmacy test."

Following the challenges that Wright overcame to reach the major leagues, something most only dream of, it was no surprise when he successfully made it through pharmacy school, graduating from Idaho State. He landed a job at a pharmacy in Utah, the state he was born in, where he, his wife, and four kids now live.

"My wife and I have a great marriage. We have great kids. I'm looking forward to grandkids, hopefully not too soon," Wright says with a laugh.

While working at the pharmacy full-time, the stocky Kamiakin High School grad isn't fully detached from the game and doesn't anticipate cutting baseball out of his life anytime soon. He still does private hitting lessons in town and hopes to potentially coach Division I college ball at some point.

"I coached college when I got back [after retiring]. The staff I was with is up at BYU right now. I would love to get back there with them," Wright said.

For now, Wright is content with what he's doing more than 16 years removed from his only major-league game. If his career had gone entirely according to plan, he might have retired just a few years ago. Wright was on the fast track to the majors, getting his first major-league call-up at 22 and was told by his organization to get comfortable, because he would be there for the next decade. But when does life ever go according to plan?

"To people who have served the country and the armed forces and come back with no legs, who am I to complain of what I have going on?" Wright said, insisting he is at peace with the way his professional baseball career turned out.

Like the perennial all-stars before his playing career and the ones who have come since he retired, Wright was one injury away from having his career vanish before his eyes. Why Wright was the one of dozens of top prospects who had his career altered in that way, nobody will ever know.

"It's hard, because you go from someone who seems invincible to someone who every muscle can break down everything, but it could have been a lot worse," Wright said. "You have two choices: you can cry about it the rest of your life or you can move on, learn from it and get better. I chose to get better."

Wright never got a hit in the major leagues. He was accountable for six outs in just three at bats in the only major-league game he ever played. Despite all that, Wright's story is one of triumph, not failure.

"It's just something that very few people ever get to do or really come close to. I was just very grateful for the time I did get up. I obviously wish it had gone a little better," Wright said.

That dream ended abruptly, but it's now something nobody can ever take away from him. When looking back on it, Wright has nothing but appreciation for what he was able to accomplish in professional baseball. Those accomplishments may pale in comparison to the expectations that 1997's no. 48 overall prospect had set for himself, but he learned something important about the game: you earn everything you get.

"A lot of times, if you have the right last name and you have a bunch of money, you can go do whatever you want," Wright said. "That's never the case in baseball. They couldn't care less."

It's baseball's cruel reality and part of its charm: nothing is ever handed to you, and even what you earn for yourself can always be taken away.

10

SAM MARSONEK

July 11, 2004

"There was just something inside my heart that I knew I was going to play in the big leagues."

Already a hard-throwing righty by the age of 12, Sam Marsonek was sure, like so many other children are at that age, of what he would do when he grew up. With his eyes on becoming one of baseball's greats, he drew inspiration from one of the best to ever put on a uniform.

"I remember cutting out an article in the paper on Ted Williams," Marsonek said. "There was a quote underneath it that said, 'All I want in life is that when I walk down the street, folks say, 'There goes the greatest hitter that ever lived.' . . . At 12, I remember scratching out 'hitter' and putting 'pitcher.' I knew that's what I wanted. I knew in my heart, that's what I was going to do." At 12 years old, he literally wrote his own destiny.

Marsonek's natural talent didn't do anything to quell his confidence. A few years after deciding he would like to be the greatest pitcher to ever live, he was dominating for Jesuit High School in Tampa, Florida. When you're 6'6", 225 pounds by your senior year of high school, you're what professional scouts like to call "projectable."

The overpowering righty knew he was good compared to the rest of the high schoolers in the country; however, scouting information wasn't as advanced in 1996 as it is now, so Marsonek wasn't sure exactly where he'd be taken in the 1996 MLB draft. Scouts had told him he might go in the third round, but he was taken much earlier than that.

With the 24th overall pick in the 1996 MLB draft, Marsonek was selected by the Texas Rangers.[1] Even at that high of a draft slot, Marsonek wasn't sure he would sign with the Rangers. He had a scholarship offer from the University of Florida, and most of the money the organization was devoting to draftees was going toward R. A. Dickey, who was drafted 18th overall the same year.

"They weren't offering me a whole lot. I was actually going to go to college. I had signed with the University of Florida. I was a day away from going to school," Marsonek said.

That's when Marsonek got a call he would never forget.

"I knew who it was, because I had a VHS [of] Nolan Ryan called *Feel the Heat* and I watched it a million times. He was definitely my hero and the person I wanted to emulate how I threw after," Marsonek said.

It was the Ryan Express. Nolan Ryan, Marsonek's idol, was on the other end of the line. That call took place late at night, as the potential future Gator recalled Ryan told him, "Hey, you need to hurry up and sign and start playing with Texas."

A phone call was great, but the money also had to get to a point where it made sense for Marsonek to turn down a full ride to play baseball at a

Sam Marsonek poses with several Latin American players spending time at his baseball camp aimed at improving baseball skills and teaching about the ministry. *Courtesy of Sam Marsonek*

school in the SEC. That was made possible after the Rangers discovered Dickey had significant UCL damage in his throwing elbow and decided to chop down their up-front financial investment in the future knuckle-baller.

After considering his options, Marsonek signed with the Rangers for $834,000 and did not attend the University of Florida.[2] Quickly, Marso-nek realized he was in over his head as a 17-year-old who had signed a contract to play professional baseball.

"One of the biggest things is, I had never dealt with failure before," Marsonek said. "Struggling early on, being a first-round pick, the expec-tations Texas had . . . none were higher than my own . . . but not knowing how to deal with failure was probably the biggest struggle for me."

A tough competitor, Marsonek pushed himself to places physically and mentally that he couldn't sustain. If he played poorly, he wanted to play well. If he played well, he wanted to play better.

"When you love the game as much as I did, and you don't perform, it's tough. It was never good enough."

To cope with failure and high expectations, Marsonek turned to some-thing he saw many others turning to early in his career: drugs and alcohol. He partied and drank his way through the pain.

"That was a way to alleviate the depression, something that ate at me all the time. I made some decisions off the field, lived a certain way, and honestly that stuff helped me sleep at night," Marsonek said.

All the partying and drinking predictably got Marsonek into trouble and earned him a label nobody wants early in their professional career.

"I drank as much alcohol as you can think about, made decisions that you make after drinking too much alcohol," Marsonek said. "I did a lot of things I wouldn't want my girls to know about. There were a lot of arrests, DUIs, fights, stuff with girls. I just made a lot of bad decisions."

The string of bad decisions began as Marsonek's career began. Right from the get-go, the newly professional ballplayer ran into issues.

"I started doing that stuff that first year in the Appalachian League. I just saw a way to deal with things and it was the only way I had seen at the time."

In Marsonek's first two seasons in professional baseball, he pitched in just 18 games. In 1999, the year he started 15 games for the Rangers' High-A ball affiliate, the Port Charlotte Rangers, he struggled, going 3–9 with a 5.54 ERA.[3] The drinking got worse.

"I think initially it was I couldn't cope with failing, or I couldn't cope with injuries and I drank. It became what I did. It became who I was," Marsonek said.

As the new millennium approached, it was threatening his professional baseball career, which had seen him pitch in just 33 games in three seasons, and he hadn't advanced past A-ball.

All it would take to get his career back on track was one team believing in the once highly touted right-hander.

On December 13, 1999, the New York Yankees traded outfielder and 1998 World Series hero Chad Curtis to the Rangers in exchange for Marsonek and fellow right-handed pitcher Brandon Knight.[4] Instantly, Marsonek knew the way the Yankees handled their players would make him more effective.

"It was like night and day from Texas to New York. Obviously, the Yankees have the history of everything, the pinstripes," Marsonek said. "The way they did things was more intentional, more professional. It felt like you mattered. It was a big deal."

Evidently, feeling like he mattered made a big difference on the mound. In 18 starts in 2000 for the Single-A Greensboro Bats, Marsonek posted a respectable 4.25 ERA to go along with a 6–7 record. While he was nowhere near major-league ready, he was showing improvement with his new organization.

The Yankees even tried to address Marsonek's well-documented off-the-field issues.

"They had stuff set up for guys like me," Marsonek said. "They made an effort to reach out to us through different avenues. Texas just brushed things under the rug. In New York, they'd say, 'If you have some issues, let's try to deal with them.'"

As much as the Yankees tried to help Marsonek get on track off the field, nothing was able to break the habits that the 6'6" righty had developed in the infancy of his professional career.

"I couldn't control it at that time. It had control of me, but I loved and respected the Yankees. I gave them everything I could, because I felt like I owed everyone around me," Marsonek said.

He especially felt like he owed Mark Newman, the Yankees' farm director. He had the utmost respect for the man who tried to give him the tools to succeed and motivated him to improve, at least between the lines.

As he continued to struggle with alcohol, Marsonek slowly started climbing the Yankees' farm system ladder. In 2001, he started 23 games for the High-A Tampa Yankees, going 8–8 with a 3.51 ERA while pitching in his hometown. That performance earned him a call to Double-A for the 2002 season, where he went 5–8 with a 5.01 ERA for the Norwich Navigators.

In 2003, the Yankees decided to start using Marsonek as a reliever instead of a starting pitcher. He started the season in Triple-A with the Columbus Clippers and pitched mainly out of the bullpen. Appearing in 54 games, Marsonek saved 18. He had built momentum going into the 2004 season, and he continued to pitch well.

"I made the [Triple-A] All-Star team that year. I had a really bad April and then I started to turn it around. In May and June, I was lights out. Everything started to click," Marsonek said.

Marsonek was now in his eighth season in professional baseball and felt he might be on his way to living out his dream, something that had been in his heart since he was 12 years old. After pushing toward that dream for a decade and a half, he could feel he was on the cusp. It was curious, then, when he was called into a meeting with coaches in which he thought he was being dealt to another ballclub.

"Right before the break, we were in Scranton and they called me into the office and I thought I was getting traded," Marsonek said.

Marsonek wasn't being traded. He was being promoted. Billy Connors, his pitching coach Neil Allen, and Bucky Dent were in the room.

"They said, 'Pack your bags, you're going to New York.' I just started bawling. I couldn't stop crying. Neil and I had spent the last four years together, so he was a mess, he was crying. Billy was crying. They had all supported me."

Marsonek made his way out into the locker room where he continued to cry and a few teammates joined him in the emotional scene. He called home, relaying the news to family through tears, thinking back on his professional career to that point.

"It was nine years, the arrests, and all the garbage, it was self-inflicted. So, that was an emotional day."

The following day, Marsonek landed in the Big Apple and had only one place he wanted to go from the airport: Yankee Stadium. It was eleven o'clock in the morning as he showed up to the House That Ruth

Built and for the first time, entered a major-league stadium as a major-league ballplayer. Security had been expecting him and let him in.

"No one was there, and of course, it wasn't yet cleaned from the night before," Marsonek said. "I just sat there. I went to the gym and worked out. I didn't want to leave. I walked into the stadium, Monument Park, I just walked everywhere. I was there all day."

After eight years of battling through problems on and off the field, Marsonek was now a member of one of sports' most iconic franchises. The greatest closer to ever live, Mariano Rivera, even teased him when he got his call to "The Show."

"I was out there throwing and he saw me and he's like, 'Man, you're finally here to take my job,'" Marsonek recalled.

Fifteen years after this conversation, Rivera became the first player in baseball history to be inducted into the Hall of Fame unanimously.

Two days after walking around Yankee Stadium for the first time as a member of the team's 25-man roster, Marsonek made his MLB debut on July 11, 2004. The Bronx Bombers were hosting the Tampa Bay Devil Rays, the expansion team from Marsonek's hometown.

"I make my debut in front of 54,000 people. It was a Sunday afternoon. My family flew up, my friends flew up," Marsonek said.

Orlando "El Duque" Hernandez was pitching a gem for New York as they built a lead on the Devil Rays. Felix Heredia replaced him and pitched into the eighth inning. With one out in the inning, the call came to the bullpen.

"The phone rings with one out and they go, 'You have the next hitter.' I think I threw three balls and went straight out to the game," Marsonek said. "It didn't matter. I couldn't feel my legs, I couldn't feel the ball. I had zero feeling."

Marsonek was being summoned with two outs in the eighth inning of a game in which the Yankees led 9–3. He trotted on to face Julio Lugo.[5]

"Coming out of the bullpen, it looked like it was literally a mile away. I was just experiencing the whole thing."

Marsonek stepped onto the mound. It felt like home. This was the moment he had thought about for the majority of his life.

"When I was 12, that's what I knew I was going to do. In that moment, there wasn't nervousness. It was 'Here's where I'm supposed to be.' . . . Finally."

Lugo swiftly hit a double off Marsonek before he could settle in. He got Damian Rolls to fly out to end the inning. Yankees manager Joe Torre decided to stick with Marsonek in the ninth as the Yankees added an insurance run in the bottom of the eighth.

After a leadoff single from Toby Hall, Marsonek sent down Geoff Blum, Carl Crawford, and Rocco Baldelli in order. Marsonek's first major-league appearance was a success; 1 1/3 innings, two hits, no runs. The outing came right before the All-Star break, and Marsonek had a discussion with Torre about what his role would be with the team going forward.

"He said, 'If you throw strikes, you finish these games that are non-save situations, you're not going anywhere.' I was going to be there through the playoffs and hopefully win a World Series," Marsonek said.

The righty never wore pinstripes again.

"I was setting stuff up, looking forward to having everybody out [for the season's second half] and then it happened."

Marsonek returned home for the All-Star break and decided to have a little fun out on the water with friends.

"I was out drinking and boating and had an accident. I blew out my knee," Marsonek said. "Just like at 12 years old, I knew I was going to be a major-league pitcher. . . . At that moment when I blew out my knee, I knew that everything was done. I knew that I would never get back."

Two days after reaching the pinnacle of his adult life, Marsonek's deep-seated habits struck down his blossoming career. The accident didn't sober him up; it made his alcohol problem worse.

"After getting hurt in 2004, I went to a deeper, darker place."

Following rehab to get his knee back to full strength, he knew it would never be 100 percent. The knee injury was something that would prove to define his career. Through the pain and rehab, though, he got back to Triple-A. It was hard for him to crawl out of the darkness the following season, once again pitching for Columbus. He appeared in 49 games and posted a career-worst 7.30 ERA.

"I went back to Triple-A in 2005 and I was lost. I was just wrecked. I couldn't figure it out. Definitely after getting hurt, after nine years of playing and finally getting called up, another bad decision took it all away," Marsonek said.

Marsonek found a chance to escape the darkness in a place where he never expected to find it: the Dominican Republic. He was asked by teammate Andy Phillips to go to the island with him following the 2005 season.

"He just said, 'We're going to go work with kids at baseball clinics and play golf,'" Marsonek said.

Coming off days of drinking, he boarded a flight for the Dominican Republic, believing it would essentially be a golfing trip with buddies. What it turned out to be was a Christian mission trip, and it altered the trajectory of Marsonek's life. Had he known the real reason for the trip at the outset, he likely never would have boarded the plane.

"I would call out all those guys when I played. I used to call them 'Chapel Guys,' but I didn't see a consistency with what they said they believed," Marsonek said.

His perception changed, though, as he arrived on the island of the Dominican Republic where the only valuable thing most children could cling to was hope.

"We were in San Pedro de Macoris, where Robinson Cano and Alfonso Soriano are from, and we just saw kids without spikes or gloves . . . there were some kids without pants," Marsonek said. "Obviously, their ticket off the island was through that game and there was so much hope in their eyes. I knew before they even started that they were never going to make it."

That harsh realization forced Marsonek, coming off a devastating, career-defining injury, to look at himself in those kids and see them as a mirror for what he was facing in the coming months and years.

"It was a weird sense of, 'We're in the same position.' Without the game, what are those kids going to do? Now here I am, yes I have a little money in the bank, but take the game away from me now and who am I? What do I have?" Marsonek remembered thinking at the time.

It was through this self-examination and through the empathy that Marsonek felt toward the Dominican children whom he taught baseball that he had found solace in a higher power.

"I went down there and everything changed; it was one of those moments where I was lost and now I'm found; I was blind, but now I see. Everything just made sense down there," Marsonek said.

Belief took Marsonek over. The trip left him profoundly changed. As he described it, life stopped being about him and started being about others.

"I came to the Lord that day and gave him everything. It was like everything was removed: all the weight, everything, my identity. I was just a changed man."

As he flew over the island on his way back to the United States, Marsonek pondered what it would be like to one day sell everything and head back to the island and help the kids he had seen.

"It was just something in my heart saying, 'I want to help,'" Marsonek said. It was that same heart, that same gut feeling telling him he would one day be a big-league baseball player too. He tucked the new thought away in the back of his mind in exchange for the old one as he began his mission to return to major-league baseball. His time with the Yankees was done. After his 2005 campaign, he was left looking for an opportunity somewhere else. Before the 2006 season, he signed with the Chicago Cubs. That door closed soon after it was opened.

"I threw my shoulder out the first day of live BP," Marsonek said. "It was just one of those moments like, 'Why now?' God had just given me everything and now you're taking away the one thing that I loved, at the time, more than anything."

Marsonek didn't pitch in professional baseball at all in 2006. By 2007, his professional baseball career had led him to the independent league, playing for the Somerset Patriots in New Jersey. Even against markedly weaker competition than what he had faced in minor-league baseball, Marsonek mustered just a 5.03 ERA in 35 appearances.

Despite his struggles over three seasons following his boating accident in 2004, the Washington Nationals decided to take a flyer on him. It looked like he had a shot of pitching at a high level again after pitching well in camp, but Washington simply didn't have any more spots left for him on any of its minor- or major-league rosters.

"I got released on the last day of camp. As soon as I got released, I just knew that was it."

Marsonek had started coaching high school ball before leaving for the Nationals' camp, so that's what he returned to after being cut.

"Prior to me leaving, those kids thought I was going to be in the big leagues that year. Going to see them after I've gotten released and knowing 'that's it,' that's humbling," Marsonek said.

For the next five years, Marsonek continued to coach high school baseball. He loved being able to influence kids after turning a corner in his life, following his trip to the Dominican Republic. But that trip kept sticking out in his mind. He wanted to make a more profound impact.

"I enjoyed it, but in high school baseball, you're just limited to the amount of kids you can work with. There's an administration and a lot of stuff to go through to get things done," Marsonek said.

MLB's no. 24 overall pick in 1996 needed a better and more efficient way to reach the kids he wanted to help through baseball and through faith. That's when, in 2012, Marsonek started a youth baseball ministry as a part of the established organization Sharing Christ Our Redeemer Enterprises (SCORE) in Tampa.

He taught life lessons through baseball to a variety of kids while at his baseball ministry through SCORE. Once again, in August 2016, he felt the need to make an even bigger impact and take an even bigger leap of faith to make it happen.

"My wife is a physician; she left the practice. I had an automotive shop. I sold the shop, sold the house and we moved out here to west Alabama, 50 acres, a couple fields, an indoor facility that can house 60," Marsonek said.

He and his family moved to Eutaw (pronounced like the state of Utah), Alabama, one of the poorest areas in the country,[6] where he set up shop with Andy Phillips, the teammate and friend who had taken him on that mission trip more than a decade earlier. It is here that he now coaches everyone from young travel ball players to professional prospects.

February through April are all about international training at Baseball Country, where kids are brought in from the Dominican Republic, Venezuela, Colombia, and Panama. This is Marsonek's busiest time of the year, where he has his biggest groups at his large facility. He describes the facility as similar to the "Field of Dreams," conjuring up images of Moonlight Graham, his cup of coffee counterpart.

"They'll work out, practice, and then play against each other in a showdown. Everything will be done here," Marsonek said.

Summers consist mostly of travel ball players coming through the facility. On top of learning baseball, they help out in Eutaw, a poor community Marsonek has felt a connection to and feels personally responsible for helping.

"In the summer, it was be predominantly American guys. We'll have some international players for those two months, but not a ton."

As the season moves to fall, high school and college team camps will roll through. On top of being taught baseball, the players are disconnected from everything to help them bond. The lack of cell service in the area helps with that mission. Those teams come in on a Thursday or Friday and stay at the facility through Sunday. A variety of activities, including skeet shooting, archery, Wiffle ball, and dodgeball are available for the kids as well. As the fun and games move out around November, the hard work begins for Marsonek and his staff. The winter is reserved for professional prospects.

"It is really catered toward our pro guys. Whether guys are coming in their offseason and training here, we basically have retreats."

Marsonek has met with major-league teams about holding retreats for some of their top prospects. He has seen interest from big-league clubs, and the momentum seems to be growing for Baseball Country.

He has developed a program for when teams send a group of their young prospects to his camp, and it revolves around three concepts: purpose, perspective, and process.

"Purpose is really about getting guys to examine their own hearts and say, 'Why are you playing the game?' If it's just about a contract or about seeing your name on TV, or girls, it's going to be too hard, because of all the ups and downs. . . . You have to have a purpose bigger than you. Using my story, bringing other guys in and their stories just provokes self-examination."

Teaching kids perspective is relatively easy for Marsonek and Baseball Country given its locale.

"Being in Eutaw, this is a place to help these guys see there are a lot of people you can influence with the platform that you're on," Marsonek said.

Process is something Marsonek is really excited about and has been working on developing for his professional players who come through. It involves pushing people to their limits so that situations in baseball don't seem difficult by comparison.

"That's really about putting them in extremely adverse situations to try and squeeze out all the garbage, pride, arrogance, lack of leadership," Marsonek said. "I'm working with six guys that are active Special Ops, high-ranking officers. We're putting a program together."

While there are many moving pieces in place for Marsonek and Co., his program at SCORE and now at Baseball Country has produced dozens of professional prospects. Many names people will know in the near future have gone through his program.

Notable alumni of his SCORE group include Eloy Jimenez, one of baseball's top prospects, a potential future star outfielder for the Chicago White Sox; Rafael Devers, a young hitter for the Boston Red Sox; and Alex Faedo, a big left-handed pitcher who became one of the top pitchers in the country at the University of Florida, the school Marsonek nearly attended.

His mission is to keep adding big names to that list and make sure the names on the list don't wander down the same road that derailed his own once-promising MLB career.

"I'm not the only guy that was like me. We're trying to get guys away from that environment and just give them an opportunity to hear something different, not in a preachy way, but in a real, transparent, open way."

Marsonek is also becoming more involved in the Eutaw community than he anticipated: he became the chaplain and receivers coach for the high school football team and actively campaigns online to raise money for equipment for the players, most of whom don't have so much as a pair of cleats. He uses his experience to help many more people than just the baseball players who come through his camp.

"I have these kids in Eutaw whose dads are incarcerated. One of my players got shot in December in a drive-by," Marsonek explained. "One of the kids came up to me after practice and said, 'Coach, I don't know what to do. My mom's relying on food stamps and there are no jobs here. What do I do? How do I make money to get food for my brothers and sisters?'"

Suddenly, Marsonek, once a total headache off the field, found himself in a position to change thousands of young athletes' lives.

While faith and a sense of a higher calling made it easier for Marsonek to walk away from the game in the end, the way his career ended up still profoundly affects him; just like any baseball player who worked his whole life toward one goal, he was torn.

"I had a complete piece of me that was like, 'Okay, that's it. The door is shut. Move on.' There was another part of me that didn't want to let go. I still wanted to try and go back."

What faith and a higher calling did give Marsonek was the ability to not *have* to go back.

"Without it, I'd probably be in independent ball or something right now," the 40-year-old said. "I don't even want to think about what I'd be doing. If I'd be alive, I have no idea. It's a scary thought, to be honest with you."

Though at a distance, Marsonek keeps all of those thoughts in his rearview mirror. He then uses them to motivate his players and keep them focused on driving their careers and lives forward, leading them away from the same what-if's he experienced during his career.

"I think that regret now is what fuels me to coach these kids. My message is: 'Your purpose has to be bigger than the game.' If baseball is the identity, there's no freedom in it. You're just restricted to your result," Marsonek said.

His transition out of the game has still been smoother than most. For many, losing the game of baseball, the only thing they've ever loved, can be crushing.

"I've had so many teammates where that transition was just awful. There are guys that stayed at home for a year, two years. They wouldn't leave the house, couldn't get a job, couldn't interact," Marsonek said. "It was just too much. To most people, it doesn't make any sense. Until it has controlled your life and it's gone, it's really hard to understand unless you did it."

The emotional toll on a ballplayer is very real when they realize there's no longer a place in the game for them. That's true even of Marsonek, who has grown emotionally and spiritually stable through his unique journey.

"There are only a few guys that can walk away from it. Everyone else, you have to take their uniform. That's the hardest thing for people to comprehend," Marsonek said. "When it's over, it's over. It's something most of these guys have been doing since they were four, five, six years old." In Marsonek's words, it isn't the sheer inability to play anymore that drives the pain. It's something more personal than that.

"There's some hurt involved when they tell you you're not needed anymore."

Marsonek is now needed in a much more important way, but even he still has trouble being away from the game. On a trip to a Braves game with a large group of his players, he flashed back to his playing days and some of the anguish associated with them.

"I had 18 guys with me. I got them all seated and I just walked around the stadium and SunTrust Park has this little monument area for Braves Hall of Famers, and just seeing that reminded me of Monument Park," Marsonek said. "I didn't make it to the second inning. I had to get out."

Marsonek left the game in the first inning, because being in a big-league ballpark reminded him so much of what could have been. While it doesn't eat away at him the way it does other players, it still poses internal questions he doesn't have perfect answers to yet.

"I think I spent my whole life trying to control a ball and I realized the ball had controlled me."

This realization and the many that would follow Marsonek's trip to the Dominican Republic may have happened too late to save his playing career, but those realizations only strengthened his overall connection to the game he loved.

"I loved the game when I was terrible. I loved the game when I was hurt. I loved the game when it didn't love me back," Marsonek said.

And now, he uses that love to teach others through the national pastime.

Life never goes according to your script, but as far as baseball goes, Marsonek got pretty close. The prophecy he set for himself at 12 years old was fulfilled, if only for a day. He pitched in a major-league game in front of 54,000 fans at historic Yankee Stadium. Everything after that? He never imagined his impact on the game could go so far beyond his blazing fastball cracking into the catcher's mitt.

His mission is now to make sure kids with similar dreams get to pitch more games at Yankee Stadium, stay on the big-league roster, and win a World Series, all things Marsonek may have been able to do if it hadn't been for his boating accident. At the end of the day, whether his players become Hall of Famers or members of the working class, all-stars or businessmen, he is simply trying to set their futures up through baseball.

"I'm trying to teach these guys to become husbands and fathers," Marsonek said. "If they become influenceable husbands and fathers, then that's what gives me the peace and gratitude from this whole thing."

The fleeting nature of his time as a big leaguer didn't end up defining Sam Marsonek's downfall; rather, it redefined what it means for a man to consider himself a success.

"Baseball is so temporary, but the impact that can be made through the game can last a player's life."

11

MATT TUPMAN

May 18, 2008

While everyone else was playing hockey or skiing in Concord, New Hampshire, Matt Tupman was focused on a different sport. Instead of facing black diamonds on the slopes, he preferred being on a plain old baseball diamond. Tupman, an avid baseball fan and player, had to go out of the state to even find adequate competition.

He would travel south from Concord to the Boston area. When he was 13 years old, he earned a spot as the starting catcher for the New England Mariners, an Amateur Athletic Union (AAU) travel ball team. With him as their starting catcher, they won an AAU national title.

"When we beat that California team for a national title, that's when I realized I could possibly do it," Tupman said.

Helping this realization along was the fact that major-league scouts were showing up to his games by his junior year of high school.

"I had the Indians, Blue Jays, and Padres starting to come out and watch," Tupman recalled. "I didn't get drafted out of high school, but they were around. I knew it could possibly happen."

The man who instilled a passion for baseball in Matt was his father. He couldn't have been happier with the direction in which Matt's baseball career was headed.

"My father loved baseball. He wasn't very good at it. In fact, he wasn't good at it at all," Tupman said. "But he loved talking baseball. He loved statistics and all that stuff. Teddy Ballgame was his favorite."

Even though the great Ted Williams was his favorite player, Tupman's father had grown up a Yankees fan. Matt, on the other hand, started rooting on the other side of the rivalry. He grew up a Red Sox fan. Matt and his father would routinely make trips to Fenway Park, a baseball cathedral, to root against each other as they watched the Yankees and Red Sox play.

Even though he was a Red Sox fan, Tupman would admire Yankees players from afar. He watched one Bronx Bomber in particular for inspiration of how he would like to play the game: "I was a left-handed hitter, so I always watched Don Mattingly hit. I loved watching him hit," Tupman said. "I also used to study Pudge [Rodriguez]. Nobody threw better than that guy."

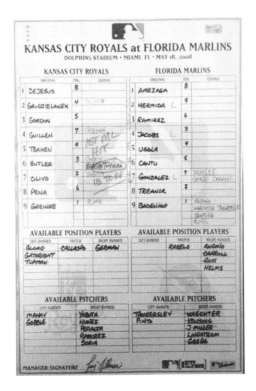

The scorecard displayed in the Kansas City Royals' dugout, the only time the card would bear Matt Tupman's name. His one career hit is denoted in red ink with "1B to RF." *Courtesy of Matt Tupman*

The stage on which Tupman himself played was getting bigger and bigger, and one trip to a tournament in Georgia changed his college prospects. As a slightly below-average student, Tupman's college options were limited.

"We went to the Babe Ruth World Series and we went down to Georgia and I got noticed by two teams in the Peach Belt Conference," Tupman said.

Out of that tournament, he got a scholarship offer from Gordon College, a small school near Barnesville, Georgia, 45 minutes outside Atlanta. He signed his letter of intent but didn't end up playing there.

"I got my ex-wife, girlfriend at the time, pregnant when I was 19, so I came home," Tupman recalled. "I came home to be with her. I gave up my scholarship to come home and be a father."

Baseball took a backseat to life, especially since Tupman was out of options at that point. He had signed his letter of intent to play at Gordon, so he had to make some concessions on where he wanted to play. Tupman ended up enrolling at Division III Plymouth State his freshman year.

"The kids weren't serious enough. They were getting wasted before the playoffs and stuff like that," Tupman said. "They didn't lift weights. It just wasn't for me."

Tupman bought himself a ticket out of Plymouth State by playing in the New England Collegiate Baseball League the following summer and meeting several people from the University of Massachusetts at Lowell. After that summer, he decided his baseball career would continue in Lowell, the hometown of famous boxer Micky Ward.[1] He enrolled at UMass-Lowell for his sophomore year.

Upon his arrival at UMass-Lowell, a powerhouse Division II program, the team reached new heights.

"They won the conference 11 straight years, but they could never get out of the regional," Tupman said. "They lost every year in the regional and never made it to the World Series. I transferred in, another kid from UMass, and a kid from Boston College also transferred in. The three of us put them over the top."

With Tupman's help, the River Hawks reached back-to-back Division II College World Series.[2] That exposure, along with his own play, helped him become the legitimate professional prospect he hadn't yet become by the time he graduated from high school. Scouts told him he would be taken between the 4th and 12th rounds of the 2002 MLB draft.

"My year was the first year the draft was ever held on the internet. The internet was just starting to come out and you could only hear it, you couldn't watch anything," Tupman explained.

The only problem for him on draft night was that he didn't own a personal computer. He was in college and couldn't just pop open a laptop and listen to the live draft results.

"PC's weren't common back then. I would have to go to the computer lab to use a computer," Tupman said.

Instead of watching on a computer, Tupman relaxed with friends as he waited for his name to potentially be called by a professional baseball team. It was the man who originally shared his passion for baseball with Matt who told him the news.

"I was at my house, just hanging with some buddies and my father called me, because he had a computer," Tupman said. "He was like, 'You just got drafted! You just got drafted!' It was pretty exciting."

Tupman was drafted in the ninth round by the Kansas City Royals, basically right in the middle of where scouts had predicted he would land.[3] The Royals were a team in disarray, going 206–279 in the three seasons before Tupman was drafted, and they were well on their way to a 62–100 season when they called his name in the MLB draft.[4] None of that mattered to Tupman.

"I was the kind of guy where I was like, 'Where do I sign?' I'll go for a plane ticket and a chance," Tupman said.

Kansas City sent out a scout for the negotiation process with the catcher from Concord, New Hampshire, their ninth-round pick. It didn't last long.

"They offered me $60,000 to leave school and I said, 'Where do I sign?' It wasn't a negotiation."

Tupman headed straight to Spokane, Washington, where he joined the Spokane Indians, the Royals' Low-A ball affiliate. His dad, retired by this time, came all the way out to Spokane from New Hampshire to spend most of the summer with his son. Matt was now being paid to play the sport his dad loved so much.

"The minor leagues are like an emotional roller coaster, especially at those lower levels, because people are gone quickly," Tupman said. "That first team I had, not many people made it really even to Double-A."

Tupman, a self-diagnosed "organizational catcher," never hit for much power but did bat .271 in his first partial professional season, ensuring he wouldn't be one of those players removed from the organization quickly. His performance was good enough to earn him a spot on the Burlington Bees in A-ball in 2003, one level up from where he had begun his career.

This meant Burlington, Iowa, would become Matt's father's new home. He spent most of Matt's first full professional season with him and watched his son hit .223 in 81 games. As he had been all of Matt's life, he was someone Matt could talk through the game with. Being such an avid fan of the game, Matt's father loved nothing more. Unfortunately, Burlington was the last stop he was able to see on Matt's professional journey.

Matt's father passed away in October, shortly after the Bees' season wrapped up.

"That was one of the most emotional things I've ever had to deal with," Tupman said.

Less than two years into his professional career, Tupman's biggest supporter was gone. It was a tough offseason for him emotionally, but he made sure to include his father on his professional journey as it continued. Even while he couldn't see what his son was doing, Matt made sure to keep him up to date.

"Every year that I played, every affiliate I went to, I would go to his grave and I would give him one of my hats," Tupman said. "I would visit him and say, 'I made it another level, Dad. You'd be so proud.'"

Tupman left several hats at his father's grave. In 2004, he gave his father a Single-A Wilmington Blue Rocks cap. By 2005, his dad had a Double-A Wichita Wranglers hat and a Surprise Scorpions hat from the Arizona Fall League. The headwear continued to roll in when Tupman earned a call-up to Triple-A in 2006. His dad got an Omaha Royals hat as a result.

Tupman played for the Omaha Royals for the remainder of 2006 and played the entire 2007 season there, hitting .281 while following that up in the Dominican winter league by hitting .293. The "organizational role player" was rising up the ranks. He also befriended Jose Guillen while in the Dominican. Guillen was a key player for a struggling Royals team and was described by Tupman as being the team's "unofficial captain."

This friendship seemed like any other formed by teammates, but it would run deeper and become a friendship that changed the course of Tupman's career.

Tupman became teammates with Guillen again sooner than he may have expected. One of the Royals' big-league catchers, Miguel Olivo, was injured as 2008 spring training drew to a close. He wouldn't be on the shelf for long, but the Royals needed to carry two catchers on their big-league roster when the season began.

"They called me into the office and go, 'Matt, you're going to make the Opening Day roster.' It was really emotional. It was surreal. It happened quickly," Tupman said. "It seemed like a long road, but at the same time, it seemed really fast."

"All of a sudden, I wished my dad was there, but he wasn't."

Tupman's lifelong dream had come true: he had made a major-league roster. Not only was he called up to the Royals, but he was one of the 25 players the organization decided to carry on its Opening Day roster. Even though he was on the Opening Day roster, he didn't get into a game before Olivo returned from his injury. He was sent back to Omaha before getting an at bat.

"The Royals had John Buck and Miguel Olivo, so they really just had two potential starters competing. They just let those two battle it out," Tupman said. "Had they had a bona fide starter, I think my chances [to be a full-time big-league backup catcher] would have actually been better."

Tupman was stuck. He wasn't quite in a situation where he could crack the major-league roster, but he was playing well enough at Triple-A to deserve a call-up. There just wasn't room for three catchers on the Royals' 25-man roster.

"It was like being in purgatory. It was tough, but that's where the mental game comes in," Tupman said. "At those levels, everyone can physically get it done, but being able to deal with the up and down, up and down, that's what can make you crazy."

It didn't take long for a "down" to turn into another "up" for Tupman, who was called up again in May when Buck, one of the Royals' two active catchers, went on paternity leave after his wife went into labor. Tupman knew, like the other time he had been up with the Royals, his time with the big-league team would be limited.

Compounding that problem was the fact that big-league manager Trey Hillman seemed to want nothing to do with him.

"I was there the first time for a week and I didn't even get one at bat, not a pinch hit, nothing," Tupman said. "Trey just did not like me. I don't know why. We just rubbed each other the wrong way."

By the time May 18 rolled around, another several days had passed without Tupman entering a game. The team was in Miami on a getaway day, a series-finale day game after a night game, which is normally a game a backup catcher might see a start in order to give the regular catcher a breather. Tupman's name was not on the lineup card. It appeared Tupman had missed his chance at getting into a big-league game again.

Tupman's mother had told him she thought he would play on May 18. Never doubt a mother's intuition.

"My mother had flown down the night before. She claimed she had this feeling I was going to play," Tupman said.

But Billy Butler, an emerging young star for Kansas City, delivered news to Tupman that would prove his mom wrong. Butler obsessively monitored the news wire to see what writers were saying about him and the team and shared some information with Tupman before the team had even arrived at Dolphin Stadium. Kansas City's backup catcher would have preferred Butler kept the information to himself.

"Hey Tup, they said they're sending you down today," Butler said.

"Why does that need to be said, man?" Tupman thought to himself, annoyed by the young Butler's antics.

The Royals were slated to play the Red Sox the next day. Worried he wouldn't be able to make the trip to Boston to take on his hometown Red Sox at Fenway Park after the game in Miami, Tupman decided to seek out Hillman, the manager with whom he did not get along, right when he got to the ballpark.

"I said, 'Listen, Trey, I am from New England and if you grew up in New England as a child and had any idea what it's like to put on a major-league baseball uniform and step into Fenway Park, that's been my dream since I was ten years old,'" Tupman told his manager.

He continued his pitch, hoping he could prove the reports of him being sent down wrong. He was hoping his manager would allow him to stay on the 25-man roster past May 18.

He went on: "Is there any way I can fly with the team and go home and be at Fenway with my family and just put on a major-league uniform and actually be a player on that field?"

Hillman's response was, "Well, I don't know."

"I basically begged him to go to Boston, to go to Fenway as a player just one time. I get goosebumps just thinking about that possibility," Tupman said.

Tupman heard nothing for the rest of the day from his manager. It was game time, and it was time for Tupman to once again sit on the bench in a major-league dugout and wonder what it would be like to get out on the field.

Two leaders of the team lobbied hard to get Tupman in the game with Hillman, who was tough to crack. They wanted to see him get in a game after spending so much time with the team and working so hard for his chance.

"Miguel [Olivo] and Jose Guillen went to the manager and said, 'Look, this kid's been up here for two weeks. You have to get him an at bat,'" Tupman recalled.

Even at the urging of Olivo and Guillen, Tupman was not put into the game. So, Guillen, the man Tupman forged a friendship with in the Dominican Republic, and Olivo, the man starting in front of Tupman, devised a plan to get him on the field.

"I was sitting there and Jose came over to me and was like, 'Hey man, you're going to go in,' and I was like, 'Yeah right, that guy's not going to play me,'" Tupman said.

Matt didn't know the plan was already in place. It was a hot May day in Miami, and Olivo went up to Hillman and claimed he had heatstroke and had to be removed from the game defensively in the ninth inning. Hillman's hand was forced. He only had one other catcher on the roster.

"Once they told me what they were going to do, I just got myself ready," Tupman said.

Tupman would hit for the pitcher in the ninth inning and replace Olivo defensively in the bottom half of the inning with the Royals leading 9–3. He was due up second and had some time to consider what his thought process would be at the plate.[5]

"I was going up there with the mind-set 'I'm either striking out or getting a hit. There's no chance I'm walking in this spot.' I was going out there aggressive. I'm going down swinging," Tupman said.

Playing at Dolphin Stadium, a field designed for football, made things even more of a whirlwind for Tupman as he came out to the on-deck circle for the start of the ninth. He couldn't even find the on-deck circle, thanks to his nerves. He got two practice swings before Mark Teahen popped out to shortstop and he was called into action.

"Everything was in slow motion. Everything. I got up to the box and did my little routine cleaning up the box with my feet and I called time-out and looked at the umpire and said, 'Look, this is my first major-league at bat ever. You have to give me a second,'" Tupman said.

"No problem, kid. No problem," Tupman recalled home-plate umpire Jerry Meals responding. He understood.

Tupman dug in to face Marlins closer Kevin Gregg, one of baseball's premier closers at the time. He had saved 32 games the season before.[6] Gregg started him off with a two-seamer away. Tupman laid off for ball one. Gregg reared up again and came after Tupman with a forkball. He hung it.

"I can still remember it. I can still see the laces on the ball. I got it and it was kind of like my 'fuck you' to Trey Hillman," Tupman said.

He laced the offering into right field for a base hit. Tupman raced to first base, and the emotions started to race once he reached the bag.

"Once I got on base, time sped up a little bit. I was overwhelmed. I didn't even know what to do. They threw the ball in for me," Tupman said.

As he reached the peak of his professional baseball career, registering a base hit in a big-league game, there was one person that came to the front of Tupman's mind. It was the man whose grave would soon be brightened by a sharp-looking Kansas City Royals hat.

"It probably would have brought him to tears," Tupman said. "I remember jogging in from first base to the dugout to get my gear and my mother was standing above the dugout. She later told me, 'Matthew, you looked like a little boy running off the field. You looked like you were in Little League. It didn't seem any different to me.'"

It was different. It was the big leagues. That joyful young player, who realized a major-league dream could become a reality when he was 13 years old, now had a major-league hit. Tupman went out and caught a clean ninth inning from pitcher Yasuhiko Yabuta as the Royals held on 9–3 to improve to 21–22 on the year.

The Royals got back to the locker room and started to wash off the muggy Miami heat as they prepared to travel north to Boston. Tupman still hadn't heard back from anyone about whether he would be on the roster when they took off to play the Red Sox.

"I'm like, 'Am I going to Albuquerque, am I going to Boston? What's going on?' No one is saying anything, so I'm getting on that plane," Tupman said. "I got on the plane and flew to Boston."

At Fenway Park the next day, Tupman was going through his pregame routine when he was informed that Buck was back from paternity leave and there wasn't a spot on the roster for him. Tupman was hours away from playing at the park he had grown up visiting with his dad, one of his heroes, but he wouldn't be in a major-league uniform at one of baseball's most historic parks on that night.

"The team secretary said, 'Here are four tickets for you, your daughter, your friend, and your wife. You need to sit in the wives section.' So, I went up to the wives section and I sat with them and watched the game," Tupman said. "That definitely adds to the bitterness. That's the type of stuff the Royals did back then."

Jon Lester was on the mound for the Red Sox that night. He faced just ten batters in his first three innings, walking one. Tupman, from the wives section, watched with his family. Lester got through the fourth and fifth innings unscathed, striking out three more. A night Tupman thought he'd be sitting in the opposing dugout was beginning to feel special. Slowly, a buzz grew among the 37,746 at Fenway Park.[7]

The sixth and seventh innings went one-two-three for the Royals' offense as well. Lester had faced just one more than the minimum through seven innings. Butler, Olivo, and Teahen went down in order in the eighth. The ballpark was buzzing. Lester was just one inning away from the 18th no-hitter in Red Sox history. Tupman continued to watch in total disbelief.

"I feel like maybe I was meant to break it up or something strange like that," he said.

Watching from the stands, he never got the chance.

Lester walked the leadoff man, Esteban German, in the ninth. He then got Tony Pena and David DeJesus to ground out in order. Lester was one out from major-league history. Alberto Callaspo stepped in as the Royals' last hope of preventing being no-hit for the second time in franchise history. The first came on May 15, 1973, against Nolan Ryan, the first of the seven he would throw in his career.[8]

Lester got ahead of Callaspo 0–2 and went right after him. His third pitch was his last of the night. Callaspo swung through it, Jason Varitek caught it, and Fenway Park erupted. The team Tupman had grown up rooting for was rushing the field, celebrating among the most joyous of baseball occasions: a no-hitter.

At the same time, he watched the franchise that drafted him, and with which he had gotten a base hit barely 24 hours earlier, walk off the field in dismay.

"I think maybe the baseball gods were looking down and saying something to Trey like, 'Maybe you should treat people better,'" Tupman said.

Tupman's bitterness toward Hillman is palpable. He doesn't mind anyone knowing what he thinks of his former manager.

"He made it very evident he didn't want to play me," Tupman said. "The Royals were awful, like, c'mon man, you can't give me a game? Playing a day game after a night game, I should have started that game [on May 18, his debut]."

His feelings toward his teammates are a completely different story. Where Tupman felt Hillman held him back from his potential, his teammates picked him up and celebrated him for registering a hit in the big leagues after putting in six seasons of work in the minor leagues.

"The players took great care of me. Those are the most important people. In life, you have bosses. Managers are just like bosses. They come and they go. Some are nice, some are mean," Tupman said. "But the way my teammates treated me was what meant the most to me. They embraced it. Every single one of those guys had that moment that I had just had. . . . They understood the gravity of the moment. They knew how important it was to a man who dreamed of being a professional baseball player to get his first hit."

Within two days of his base hit for the Royals, he was back with Triple-A Omaha. After Lester's no-hitter, he went back to the minor leagues, where he struggled through a shoulder injury. He batted .229 in Triple-A and decided the shoulder pain was too much to keep dealing with. After the 2008 season, he decided to have shoulder surgery.

"Before I was even off the anesthesia, they had already taken me off the 40-man roster," Tupman said. "So, that was the writing on the wall right there. As I went under, they took me off the 40-man. They just totally stuck it to me."

Tupman was surprised to be included on the 40-man roster to begin with. This made him ineligible to be taken by another team in MLB's Rule 5 draft, which allows teams to select players from other team's farm systems if that player is not on the franchise's 40-man roster. If the selected player makes the team's Opening Day roster, he stays with that franchise. If he does not make the Opening Day roster, he is returned to the team he was selected from.

Tupman feels being put on the 40-man roster was a way to make sure he didn't get a chance to be a big-league backup catcher somewhere else. Being selected by another team didn't even seem like a possibility to Tupman, though.

"I feel like there was collusion. I'm a nobody, I was a backup catcher from the beginning. Who's going to take me in the Rule 5 draft?" Tupman remembered asking himself at the time.

He came back from the shoulder surgery and missed a month of the 2009 season, which he split between Double-A and Triple-A, hitting a combined .256 in just 59 games. Another player, J. R. House, was getting most of the playing time in Triple-A, making Tupman the second or third option at that level.

"Within one year, it was a complete turnaround," Tupman said. "Now, I'm the third catcher that doesn't play in Triple-A? What the hell is going on here?"

Tupman went back to the Dominican winter league after the 2009 season to try to get ready for the 2010 season, one where he might get a chance with another team.

Then, minor-league officials came to drug-test him.

In 2006, the Major League Baseball Players Association implemented a new collective bargaining agreement, which called for a stricter drug policy in the minor leagues. Before then, minor-league players were rarely tested.

"I literally went from 2002 to 2006 without getting tested once, so I could've done steroids the entire time and no one would've said a word," Tupman said.

It wasn't steroids he got busted for in 2006, though. It was marijuana. That was his first offense. His second offense came in the 2009 offseason while playing in the Dominican Republic. Those minor-league officials came and tested him, and the results came back positive for marijuana again.

"I cleaned it up after 2006 and I never smoked during the season, but I dabbled in it in the offseason," Tupman said. "It's an opinion-based thing, but I never did it while playing, obviously."

Whether or not he did it while playing didn't matter. Tupman's second positive test earned him a 50-game suspension, which effectively ended his hopes of ever getting back to the major leagues. Since he was not on a roster, he could not just wait 50 games and say he had served his suspension. He had to be on an active minor-league roster for the suspension to count.

Knowing he was facing a 50-game suspension, no franchise wanted to sign him. He sat out the entire 2010 season without a team. It was the first time in nearly a decade he wasn't playing professional baseball. By the 2010 offseason, he felt he had paid a fair price for testing positive for marijuana a second time.

"I petitioned the Commissioner's Office and said, 'I just sat out an entire season for marijuana. You have so much more serious stuff going on. Can you reinstate me?'" Tupman said.

The league granted his request, deeming the 142-game suspension he had ended up serving for his positive marijuana test was punishment enough. They reinstated him.

"After that, I basically called every person that I knew," Tupman said.

He wasn't having any luck catching on anywhere, though, as the 31-year-old looked for a way back into professional baseball.

"They wanted nothing to do with me."

Tupman wasn't offered any minor-league contracts for the 2011 season, so he decided to play in the independent league to stay in pro ball. Some one-game players have decided to exit the game with grace, taking a token of their efforts and moving on toward validation in other arenas of life. Tupman decided that for him, there could be no grace in surrender. He was, after all, a ballplayer.

"I landed with a team in the Atlantic League called the Lancaster Barnstormers. That was the last hurrah," Tupman said.

Tupman's professional baseball career ended less than 100 miles from where it began. After playing professional baseball in nine seasons, spanning ten years, he was ready to walk away from the game after 57 contests with the Barnstormers.

"I was just tired of the grind. I had been through it, so I knew what I was getting into," Tupman said. "I was a good self-evaluator, so I knew what I was. I knew I was done with the grind."

That grind included things every long-term minor leaguer is familiar with: terrible travel schedules, worse food, and less-than-stellar facilities.

"We had long bus rides. We used to call the bus the 'Iron Lung.' When I was in Double-A, we had 15-hour bus rides from Wichita to Corpus Christi and San Antonio," Tupman said. "We had food spreads with old lunch meat, peanut butter and jelly sandwiches. There would be water running through the dugout and moldy clubhouses."

Those experiences have hardened Tupman's view of professional baseball. He has even shared that outlook with prospect Ben Bengtson, one of the hitters he has worked with as an instructor. Bengtson was selected by the Pirates in the 23rd round of the 2017 MLB draft.

"Talking to a nine- or ten-year minor leaguer can be bitter. It's a different take on things," Tupman said. "He's [Ben Bengtson] all hoorah right now, and I'm like, 'Give yourself five, six years, bud. Your whole view of everything is definitely going to change.' . . . I had a song I used to walk up to in the minor leagues. It was "Boulevard of Broken Dreams" by Green Day. You start to realize what the song is about and that we're in a boulevard of broken dreams. This whole minor-league thing is all broken dreams."

He reached the major leagues and recorded a hit in his only major-league at bat. Thinking on what he believes he could have accomplished if given more of a chance, Tupman's career doesn't have much closure to it.

"I would say my career is more of a broken dream. People looking in at it would say, 'You know what, you achieved what you wanted to do, Matt,' but I lived it and it really isn't what I wanted to achieve. I think I could have done more with an opportunity," Tupman said.

However, his opinion on his career is more nuanced than that. He didn't reach the heights he wanted to for as long as he wanted to, but there are aspects of his career he appreciates to this day. Had he never gotten a major-league at bat, the eventual outcome of his career would have been a much harder pill to swallow.

"It softened the blow. I had achieved major-league status. My claim to fame is I have a 1.000 career batting average," Tupman said. "It softened the blow, because I got there. I think it would have been more bitter if I had never made it, but I did make it. That made it better."

While the long bus rides and life in the minor leagues wore on Tupman, his experience is one he wouldn't change. His outlook on how he ultimately did professionally sounds bitter, but he described his overall experience in professional baseball as a positive one.

"It's more sweet than bitter. I didn't come out of the game with a lot of money, but my intention was never to make money," Tupman said. "I've always been like a kid and I got to play a game in college. I got to play a game for another nine, ten years after college. I met a ton of people, I traveled the entire country. I got to travel internationally. The game of baseball has been great to me."

Tupman didn't make millions of dollars in professional baseball, so he has had to work for a living, something the vast majority of professional ballplayers have to do right when they leave the game. That doesn't mean he wishes he took a different life path.

"Would I trade in the experience for anything? I really wouldn't. It was such a great time traveling. I would never trade it in for anything," Tupman said.

Memories are some of Tupman's most prized possessions from his professional baseball career. He does, however, have the bat from his only game. Thanks to his hard work, his die-hard baseball fan father has a Royals hat with him always, and a son who made good on his baseball dream.

Tupman also has the ball he lined into right field on May 18, 2008. He can still see the laces in his head, realizing anew for the thousandth time that Kevin Gregg hung the forkball as he closes his eyes and takes a hack. Every time he opens them, the ball lands on the right-field grass, just as it had following the only swing of his major-league career.

12

OTHER "CUP OF COFFEE" STORIES

THE ULTIMATE SACRIFICE

Like Sam Marsonek, Ryan Spaeder idolized Ted Williams as a child. However, without the ability to hit the baseball like the greatest hitter who had ever lived, he had to emulate "Teddy Ballgame" in a different way.

"When I was growing up, I wanted to be Ted Williams, but I couldn't hit, so instead I did his second career. He was a marine, so I went with that," Spaeder said.

Spaeder knew from an early age that military service was his calling, and he dedicated himself to serving his country before he even got to high school.

"I always wanted to be a marine and I never considered being anything else but a marine since I was 13 or 14 years old," Spaeder said.

However, when Spaeder's parents offered to pay for his college once he finished up his high school work near Drexel Hill, Pennsylvania, it was hard to turn down. Instead of enlisting in the marines out of high school, Spaeder attended Penn State University and, upon graduation, took a job in the corporate world. Within a couple years, he was quickly rising through the ranks, eventually becoming a senior hedge fund manager.

Even while making a more-than-comfortable living, he wasn't getting all he wanted out of that life. After three and a half years in corporate

America, he decided to enlist in the marines as he had always said he would.

"One thing that bothered me is that I always said I was going to serve my country and I never did," Spaeder said. "I was 24 or 25 and at that point, you're an old man in the marine corps."

Nonetheless, Spaeder enlisted and during his downtime while serving his country as a marine, he carved out a niche for himself spreading interesting baseball stats and facts through social media. He built a substantial Twitter following, which he parlayed into writing gigs with NBC Sports and the *Sporting News*. He also ended up writing a book titled *Incredible Baseball Stats* with coauthor Kevin Reavy. The two needed to dedicate the book to someone. They racked their brains. They couldn't come up with anything that satisfied both of them.

Then, Spaeder came up with the idea: dedicate the book to the only two major-league players who lost their lives in World War II, Elmer Gedeon and Harry O'Neill. That's where our story of Harry O'Neill begins.

O'Neill was born on May 8, 1917, in Philadelphia. It wasn't long before he was one of the standout athletes in the area, excelling at baseball, basketball, and football. Although basketball seemed to be his best sport, baseball offered him the most opportunity. After an incredible prep career at Darby High School, O'Neill went on to become one of the most decorated athletes in the history of Gettysburg College. There, he was a three-sport athlete, catching for the baseball team and playing center for both the basketball and football teams. After such a notable college career, O'Neill was sought after by many clubs, but only seriously considered two: the Washington Senators and the Philadelphia Athletics.[1]

While there were rumors at the time he was going to sign with the Senators, the "Grand Old Man of Baseball" Connie Mack convinced him to sign a contract for $200 a month with the Athletics. O'Neill signed on June 5, 1939, exactly one week before Connie Mack was enshrined in Cooperstown during the opening of the National Baseball Hall of Fame, marking the 100th anniversary of the first baseball game in the country's history.

From the moment he signed, O'Neill was entangled in baseball history. As soon as he signed with his hometown Athletics, he became the team's third-string catcher, traveling with the club but never playing. Finally, on a hot summer day, July 23, 1939, O'Neill was put into a major-league game. Connie Mack had become ill, so his son, Earle Mack, was managing the ballclub and decided to give regular catcher Frankie Hayes a rest from the sweltering heat with Philly down big to Detroit late in the game.

Down 15–3 in the bottom of the eighth, O'Neill entered the game as a defensive replacement. He caught the eighth inning, recording neither a putout nor an assist. He did not bat in the top of the ninth inning as his Athletics lost in a blowout. That was the first and only time he would appear in a game with the A's. He did, however, play for the A's the very next day in an exhibition game against the Penn Athletic Club in Cooperstown on "Connie Mack Day." Philly won the game, 12–6. O'Neill was released by the Athletics in September, three months after signing with them. He didn't pursue a contract with another club.

He was hired onto the faculty at Upper Darby Middle School back in his hometown, where he taught history and coached three different sports. During this time, O'Neill also played semiprofessional basketball for the Harrisburg Caissons. He played for the Caissons during the winter between 1939 and 1940 as well as the following winter. Between those two stints, he tried his hand at baseball one more time, appearing in just 16 games for the Class B Harrisburg Senators in 1940 before walking away from professional baseball for good. Ever the athlete, O'Neill also played football for Clifton Heights in 1941. Another event in 1941 changed the course of his life and of baseball history.

On December 7, 1941, when the Japanese attacked Pearl Harbor, it became only a matter of time until American boys were sent overseas by the thousands. O'Neill enlisted with the marines in September 1942 and began his training. He was 25 years old, the same age as Spaeder, when he answered his call of duty.

"It just blew my mind what this guy had done, what this guy had given up. Of course, he had his one appearance," Spaeder said. "As I looked more and more into it, I thought, this guy is Moonlight Graham."

As Spaeder continued learning about O'Neill's story, he read about his training in Quantico, Virginia, and about his deployment to Japan in January 1944. O'Neill made assaults on Kwajalein, Saipan, and Tinian. According to a newspaper story from the time, O'Neill's shoulder was injured by shrapnel in Saipan in July 1944. For this, he received the Purple Heart. Within three months, he was back on active duty.

His assignment by February 1945 was to go with the 25th Marine Regiment to Iwo Jima, one of the deadliest war zones in the Pacific. On March 6, 1945, while trying to gain every yard of battleground they could, O'Neill's regiment came under sniper fire. O'Neill was shot through the throat. The bullet severed his spine, and he died immediately.[2]

Spaeder's spirits were down at the time he was reading about O'Neill's story. Through his research, he gained some perspective.

"When I found out all this about Harry, it was like a rebirth. I thought, 'How can I possibly be complaining about what I had to give up?'" Spaeder asked. "This guy gave up all that and more: he died. . . . In reading Harry's story, I again felt like this was something I had to do. He's the reason why."

It took a month for news to reach O'Neill's family. Devastated, his sister, Susanna, wrote a letter to Gettysburg College, where he had been one of the most accomplished athletes in school history, saying:

> Our hearts are very sad and as the days go on, it seems to be getting worse. Harry was always so full of life, that it seems hard to think he's gone. But God knows best, and perhaps someday, we will understand why all this sacrifice of so many fine young men.[3]

After the war ended, major leaguers who had missed some of their prime years returned home for the 1946 season. O'Neill and Elmer Gedeon, a pilot in the army air corps who was killed in action in 1944, are the only former major leaguers to die in World War II, the only ones not given a chance to come back and compete for roster spots.

"So often, we use Ted Williams or Joe DiMaggio as these great symbols of sacrifice, but truthfully during World War II, Joe DiMaggio played baseball and Ted Williams was in training," Spaeder said. "Those are the guys you always hear about, but here are these guys I'd never heard of until I started looking into it."

As Spaeder pointed out, Williams did eventually develop a deep sense of patriotism, serving in the Korean War, costing him two more years of his career. However, he and DiMaggio, the sport's top stars at the time of World War II, are always looked at as the symbols of baseball's sacrifice to war. DiMaggio and Williams lost seasons; Gedeon and O'Neill lost their lives.

"There are any number of players who would have been willing to make the same sacrifice, but they were fortunate enough to come home. These guys weren't," Spaeder said.

As Spaeder continued reading about O'Neill's story, he realized his connection went beyond baseball and beyond the marine corps. O'Neill is buried in Arlington Cemetery in Drexel Hill, Pennsylvania, where Spaeder grew up. He attended the rival middle school to Spaeder's middle school. Spaeder had grown up idolizing Ted Williams, not knowing another potential idol was buried right up the road from him.

"When I found out Harry O'Neill was buried in Arlington Cemetery, I took my best friend, Charlie, on a hunt trying to find his headstone. After a while, we finally found it and all you could see was 'ink O,' because his name is 'Harry Mink O'Neill,'" Spaeder said. "It was so covered up, nobody had been there in years, so I'll go back once a year and Charlie goes back periodically to make sure his headstone is cleaned off. . . . Whenever we go by, we leave him a beer. That's a big thing in the service. Guys will go visit the graves of their buddies who have passed on and they leave a beer instead of flowers, because they don't want flowers," Spaeder laughed.

Although O'Neill died decades before Spaeder was born, he grew to feel like he knew him personally. His story was so close to his own, and the timing of his enlistment in the marines was nearly identical. Using his platform and growing following, Spaeder has attempted to bring Gedeon and O'Neill "back to life" by telling people their stories.

"For me to visit Harry's grave and you can't even see the name on there, it broke my heart. I'm not saying these guys deserve a plaque in the Hall of Fame, but their stories should be known," Spaeder said. "It symbolizes what these guys gave up. It's the ultimate sacrifice."

Through people like Spaeder, touched by O'Neill's life in baseball and in the armed forces, O'Neill's story lives on. He's the only cup of coffee player to be killed in World War II. For that reason alone, he will always be remembered. Unlike many players in this book, he didn't have the time to worry about what his career after baseball would be; he felt the marines were his calling.

Eddie Collins is baseball's all-time leader in sacrifices with 512[4] and was also willing to put his life on the line for his country; he served in World War I.[5] However, on March 6, 1945, Harry O'Neill laid down one of the two greatest sacrifices in the history of Major League Baseball.

BASEBALL'S FIRST STRIKE

One of baseball's most peculiar, and frankly, hilarious days was precipitated by one of its most famous early stars. Ty Cobb, despised by fans, opponents, and teammates alike, finally crossed the line by climbing into the stands during a May 15, 1912, game against the New York Highlanders. He had been pestered all game by a relentless heckler, Claude Lueker, who happened to be missing one whole hand and three fingers on the other. Despite his handicap, and because of the reaming he had been giving Cobb all afternoon, the Georgia Peach wailed on the man as people shrieked in disgust.

Ban Johnson, president of the American League, was in attendance that day and was horrified by what he saw. His front-row seat for the altercation compelled Johnson to suspend Cobb indefinitely. He heard no explanation from Cobb about the incident and did not give the Tigers star a chance to defend himself. Thanks to this, baseball's first organized strike was born.

Miffed by Johnson's unilateral decision-making in his punishment of Cobb, the Tigers players said they would strike and not play if the Peach was not reinstated. This decision was made after their game on Friday, May 17. If the Commissioner's Office didn't relent, the Tigers would have nobody to play for them on May 18 in Philadelphia against Connie Mack's Athletics, the defending World Series champions.

Faced with a fine of $5,000 if they didn't field a team that day, manager Hughie Jennings was told to find anyone he could. The Tigers needed a backup plan and replacement players in case the regulars stuck to their word. Detroit's owner Frank Navin knew a 20-year-old college junior at St. Joseph's College nearby, whom he enlisted to help recruit players for the game that afternoon. The man's name was Allan Travers, and he was the one who put together the ragtag group that was Detroit's "plan B" that day.

By the time he got everyone to Shibe Park for the game, Travers had recruited eight other players, two of them local amateur boxers and the other six random players with only college or semiprofessional experience. Each player was to be paid $25 for his time. At first, it appeared they might not be needed. They were seated behind the Detroit bench as the regulars took the field. However, Ty Cobb sprinted out to center field with the rest of the team. When he was ordered off the field, the rest of the team joined him.

Rather than lose $5,000 to a forfeit, the fine for such an offense in 1912, Jennings called on his replacement players to take the field. They put on the uniforms of the Tiger regulars and went to their positions. An offering of $50 was made to whoever was willing to pitch that day. Travers jumped at the opportunity, although he later said he had never pitched before in his life.[6] With that, a 20-year-old who had never pitched a baseball took the mound against the defending World Series champions.

His battery mate was 48-year-old Deacon McGuire, who was working as a scout for Detroit, and was asked to come out of retirement for the game. He debuted in the big leagues in 1884 and played in every season from then until 1910, excluding 1909. He came back for one final appearance. He was joined by fellow Detroit scout Joe Sugden, who last played in the big leagues seven years earlier and took the field at first base at 41 years old.

Eight players who saw action in the game—Travers, Hap Ward, John "Cup of" Coffey (playing under the alias "Jack Smith"), Dan McGarvey, Jim McGarr, Vincent Maney, Bill Leinhauser, and Ed Irwin—were playing in the only major-league game of their careers.

Almost unbelievably, third baseman Billy Maharg (actually Graham; he spelled it backward as an alias), who made his debut at 31 years old, ended up playing one more game in his major-league career, four years later with the Philadelphia Phillies in 1916.

It's for the best. "Moonlight Maharg" doesn't have the same ring to it.

In his career, he played in two games, separated by four years, and got just one at bat in each. He never recorded a hit. He did, however, play a prominent role in the 1919 Black Sox scandal as a gambler.

The legendary Connie Mack was annoyed with the entire situation and didn't want his powerhouse Athletics to take it easy on Detroit. Instead, he ordered them to go 100 percent. They obliged.

It made for one of the most lopsided games in the history of the sport. Even though the game was just 6–2 Athletics through four innings, Philly turned on the jets the rest of the game. The team bunted for base hits left and right and relied on the Tigers to beat themselves (which they did, committing nine errors).

McGarr got the platinum sombrero, going 0-for-4 with four strikeouts. Leinhauser, one of the aforementioned boxers and Cobb's replacement in center field, wasn't much better, going 0-for-4 with three strikeouts. Those results make sense considering the A's threw Jack Coombs and Herb Pennock at them. Each was an ace at the time, and Pennock is now in the Hall of Fame.

Travers labored on the mound through the entire afternoon in front of a surprisingly large, 20,000-fan crowd at Shibe Park. The Athletics knocked him around, and he certainly wasn't helped by his defense. By the time the carnage was through, Travers had pitched eight innings (a complete game since the Tigers were on the road) and given up 26 hits and 24 runs, only 14 of them earned. Those 24 runs are still the most runs given up by a single pitcher in a nine-inning game in baseball history.

While it was likely exhilarating for the six one-game wonders who took the field that day, it became clear that they were simply being used to save the team from their $5,000 fine. At least they got to be a part of baseball history.

Travers, on top of being the record holder for most runs allowed in a nine-inning game, is the only eventual Catholic priest to ever pitch in a major-league game. He entered the ministry in the years following the contest.

This game produced the most cups of coffee in major-league history with eight players calling it their only major-league game. The lone bright spot among them was Irvin, a 30-year-old catcher and third baseman. Amazingly, he went 2-for-3 with two triples, good enough for one of baseball's best cup of coffee performances ever. As expected, though, the Tigers lost the game 24–2.

Following one of the most ridiculous games in the history of the sport and worried his teammates might get fined if they continued to strike, Cobb gave them the go-ahead to keep playing. It was a rare show of selflessness from the Georgia Peach. Each player who participated in the strike was fined $100. Cobb was given a ten-day suspension.

So, the most prolific day in the history of cup of coffee players was brought on by the fire and fury of baseball's most temperamental superstar. Without Cobb's rampage in the stands and Ban Johnson's reaction to it, there would be eight fewer players in the history of baseball, none of them able to tell the crazy story about the one day they suited up to get whooped by the defending World Series champs.

BERT SHEPARD'S AMAZING JOURNEY

Kevin Keating, a military veteran and baseball memorabilia collector, walked eagerly up the steps to the Washington Hotel around the corner from the White House. Soon, he knew, he would be seeing the man he referred to as a second father: Hall of Famer Warren Spahn. Keating and Spahn had befriended each other long before and were joining up before a dinner aimed at raising money for a planned World War II memorial.

It was Thursday, November 9, 2000. George W. Bush had won the presidential election two days prior, although that would not be decided until much later. The country, without knowing it, was less than a year away from being plunged into another war. On this night, though, among the celebrated guests were the greatest generation. On top of Spahn, Buck O'Neil and Bob Feller were also in attendance.

Keating walked into the hotel lobby and was greeted by Spahn. The two close friends walked downstairs to the restaurant ahead of the dinner reception to follow. As the two talked, up walked another former major leaguer also on the guest list.

"Hello, I'm Bert Shepard," the man said to the duo, introducing himself.

Spahn didn't know who he was. Keating did. Bert sat down with the two, and it quickly became clear to Keating that Shepard was not going to tell his own story. So, Keating enlightened his friend, one of the game's greatest pitchers.

"Warren, Bert was injured in World War II. He lost a foot," Keating said. "Despite that, he pitched in the major leagues."

"You pitched after that?" Spahn bellowed in disbelief.

"Yes, I did, actually," Shepard responded. "I pitched in one game."

In order to properly inform Spahn and give Shepard his due, Keating had to back up. At some point, Shepard took over and told his story, Keating hearing it for the first time in the man's own words.

Robert "Bert" Shepard was born into what would become a very competitive household on June 28, 1920, in Terre Haute, Indiana. At the time, he was the youngest of two boys. By the time the Shepards were done, and God bless them, they had six sons. Naturally, these sons were competitive with one another in sports, but Bert was regarded as the most gifted.[7]

The Great Depression hit the Shepard family hard, forcing Bert's father, John, out of his delivery business and into work as a laborer. By the time Bert was ten years old, he was sent to live with his grandmother in Clinton, Indiana. It was here, SABR researcher Terry Bohn notes, that Shepard had his first major baseball memory. He vividly recalls listening to the St. Louis Cardinals playing in the 1931 World Series on his grandma's radio.[8]

His love for baseball burned hotter as he played semiprofessionally in high school. Clinton had no high school baseball team. Eventually, Shepard convinced himself he had what it took to play at the pro level. He moved to California, continuing to play baseball on Sundays with locals. The southpaw was impressive enough to get chatter about him to reach pro scouts' ears.

He was signed by the Chicago White Sox for $60 a month in 1939. After two seasons with Chicago, where he reached as high as the Class D Wisconsin State League with the Wisconsin Rapids, Shepard was released. His control problems assured the White Sox he would never reach the major leagues. In 43 innings, he walked 48 batters.

Shepard took a year off to get his high school diploma, which he did in 1940, and returned to Organized Baseball the following season. He pitched for multiple teams across 1941 and 1942 in the St. Louis Cardinals' farm system, the brainchild of Branch Rickey, one of the pioneers of the modern minor leagues, and the man who eventually signed Jackie Robinson. Shepard again struggled with his control.

With World War II raging overseas, there would soon be new targets Shepard was tasked with hitting. Along with millions of his fellow Americans, Shepard enrolled in the military. He enlisted in the air force early in 1943 as the war effort heated up. Hundreds of major leaguers and thousands of minor leaguers joined the cause. According to SABR research, Shepard was flying among the first Allied planes to go over Berlin in the daytime. That was in March 1944. A couple of months later, on May 21, the Allied forces planned a large-scale attack near Hamburg, Germany.

Although Shepard was supposed to pitch for his military baseball team that day, he volunteered to be part of the mission. He should have been on the mound, but he instead took to the air. The mission had gone well, and Shepard turned back. Before arriving safely for the game he was supposed to play in, he faced enemy fire. Before he knew what was going on,

Shepard was shot in the right leg and the chin. The shot to his lower body ripped through his leg and foot. The shot that clipped his chin knocked him unconscious, sending his plane hurtling toward the ground.

His plane made impact with the ground going nearly 400 miles per hour. In the first miracle of Shepard's unbelievable story, he survived the impact of the crash. German farmers wanted to kill him but were held back at gunpoint, forced backward. Shepard's life was saved by a German physician and two armed soldiers, but he became a prisoner of war. Due to the damage that had been done by the aircraft fire, German doctors amputated the bottom 11 inches of his right leg, the drive leg for a left-handed pitcher. He was fitted for a prosthetic and began throwing baseballs again once he felt comfortable wearing it.

Shepard spent eight months as a prisoner of war and was turned back over to the United States through a prisoner exchange in February 1945. Upon returning to Clinton, Indiana, where he had previously played in the minors, he wanted to show he could still make it in professional baseball. The pitcher whose control issues had derailed his career to that point, now pitching with one leg, felt he had what it took.

It was through a chance encounter with a high-ranking military official that Shepard's life changed and the history of baseball was impacted. Undersecretary of War Robert Patterson visited Shepard when he was being fitted for a new prosthetic in Washington, D.C. Patterson delivered him a commendation for his courage and service in the war. Something else Patterson gave him would mean even more: a chance.

While the two were talking, Patterson asked Shepard about his goals. His response: to play professional baseball. Patterson could have dismissed the notion as impossible. Instead, he placed a call to his friend, Clark Griffith, the owner of the Washington Senators. After hearing Shepard's story from Patterson, Griffith decided to let him try out for the team. Days after receiving his new prosthetic leg, Shepard went to College Park, Maryland, to try out for the Senators.

With little chance of being tabbed as anything more than a batting-practice pitcher, Shepard opened some eyes at his tryout. Since his left leg, the only one still whole after the war, had been left unharmed, he was still able to balance. He looked comfortable in his prosthetic, and it was hard to tell he was even wearing one. Less than three weeks after his tryout, the Senators signed him to a major-league contract. Once he regained his control in the minor leagues, he would join the big-league club.

On July 10, Shepard pitched in an exhibition game where he gave up just one hit and no runs while pitching into the fourth inning. Washington had seen all it needed to see. The Senators added him to their active roster following the dazzling performance. For several weeks, Shepard pitched batting practice for the Senators while continuing to pitch well in exhibition games. His war-hero status was solidified as he toured veteran hospitals at home and on the road with Washington.

Fatigue caught up with the Senators by August 4, 1945. There were 13,000 fans at Griffith Stadium for the second game of the doubleheader between the Senators and Red Sox, a 3:51 p.m. first pitch. It was Washington's fourth straight doubleheader. The game moved quickly, 2–2 heading into the fourth inning. After sending 15 batters to the plate, Boston had scored 12 runs and opened up a 14–2 lead. Following several weeks of sitting in the Washington bullpen, Shepard was called into mop-up duty.

He was summoned to face George "Catfish" Metkovich with a runner on second and two outs. Mercifully, he struck Metkovich out and stopped the bleeding. Shepard became the first major leaguer to play with a prosthetic leg. He wasn't done.

Shepard trotted back out for the fifth inning. He didn't have to face the heart of the Boston order, which included Ted Williams and Dom Di-Maggio, because those guys were still serving in the military. Instead, the Red Sox had a watered-down roster akin to most in the league during World War II. Leon Culberson led off the inning by reaching on an error. Shepard's control issues reared their ugly head again; he hit Pete Fox, giving Boston runners on first and second with no outs. Skeeter Newsome grounded into a double play and Bob Garbark flew out to center field. Just like that, Shepard was through 1 1/3 scoreless innings.

The one-legged pitcher went back to the mound to pitch the sixth inning, still down 14–2. A walk, sac fly, and single later, he had yielded his first major-league run, allowing Boston to extend the lead to 15–2. That was the only damage they would do that inning, though, as Shepard pitched his way out of trouble again.

Shepard's performance quickly became the story of the day. He pitched a scoreless seventh and eighth inning, allowing him to go out and finish up his outing in the ninth. In Boston's final at bat, Tom McBride grounded out on a ball that skipped off Shepard and right to second baseman Fred Vaughn, who threw to first baseman George Blinks for out number one. Metkovich got revenge for his earlier strikeout as he slugged a one-out base hit. Culberson was next and grounded into a 6-4-3 inning-ending double play. Shepard had pitched 5 1/3 innings on one leg and had given up just one earned run. He even appeared at the plate four times for the Senators, walking once. Washington lost 15–3.

It is among the most unlikely performances in MLB history. Less than six months after being released as a prisoner of war, a man with one leg, who survived being shot out of the sky, hitting the ground in an aircraft going almost 400 miles an hour, and being pursued by a throng of German farmers who wanted to kill him, had just pitched one heck of a game at baseball's highest level.

Two days after his epic pitching performance, the United States dropped the first atomic bomb on Hiroshima, the beginning of the end of World War II.

Shepard's performance would have earned him more major-league playing time had he pitched in the few years leading up to 1945. Just like most cup of coffee players, though, the timing of Shepard's ascent was poor. The Senators had finished in the bottom three of the American League in three of the past four seasons, but 1945 presented a chance for Washington to make a rare run at the pennant. They were locked in a close race with the Tigers atop the standings. Manager Ossie Bluege didn't want to be known as the coach who put a one-legged pitcher in and lost the team a pennant.

Shepard didn't pitch in another game in 1945 as a result, and the Senators fell 1 1/2 games short of the Tigers for the AL pennant. Detroit went on to beat the Cubs in the fall classic, the last one Chicago would play in for another 71 years. Before that series was even played, Shepard was released by the Senators. Again, Washington fell into the cellar of the American League. As star players returned from the war to join other American League teams, the Senators failed to climb above the .500 mark in any of the next three seasons and finished in seventh place out of eight twice.

The determined lefty was still set on making his major-league dream a more prolonged reality. He tried out for the Senators once again during spring training of 1946, but predictably, there was no spot for him. Major-league regulars had come back from the war. He requested to be sent down to the minor leagues to play after coaching for the Senators. His request was granted, but he struggled with his control once again. Soreness in the bottom of his stump forced him to get more of his leg removed via surgery.

Ever determined, Shepard continued to play baseball, if nothing else, to prove he could. Over the next decade, he played for a St. Louis Browns farm club, a semiprofessional team, and several teams in various leagues in the early to mid-1950s. Shepard retired after the 1955 season in which he played in a few games for the Modesto club in the California League. After that, he befriended future Hall of Fame shortstop Phil Rizzuto. The Yankee legend and Shepard became golfing pals.

One time, recalling a time he had faced him in spring training, Yogi Berra told Shepard, "You would've been a pretty good pitcher if you hadn't lost that leg." Berra didn't realize he had faced Shepard *after* he'd been reduced to one good leg.

As Shepard became a decorated golfer on the amputee tour, years turned into decades. Nearly five decades after he had been spared from the German farmers who wanted to kill him, Shepard continued to wonder who had saved his life. In 1993, Ladislaus Loidl, the physician in the field that day, was on a hunting trip with a British businessman in Hungary. The businessman knew of Shepard, and after hearing Loidl's story about the rescue mission 49 years earlier, he urged him to reach out to the man whose life he saved.

Loidl listened to the advice, and the two men arranged to meet in May 1993 at Loidl's home in Austria. The story quickly spread and was the subject of *This Week in Baseball*, who Sheppard told, "I prayed for this. After half a century, my dream has incredibly come true."

That wasn't his only incredible dream come true. Loidl made the other dream possible by saving him. After that, Shepard's determination to reach the majors, against all odds, powered him to one of baseball's most impressive pitching performances ever. He stood on a major-league mound just once in his career, but in a life as interesting and improbable as his, Shepard was fortunate to have even one day. Two of his best days came half a century apart: the day he pitched out of trouble for the Senators and the day he met the man who helped him get there.

CLOSING THOUGHTS

"**B**aseball is 90 percent mental. The other half is physical."

One of Yogi Berra's many famous quotes does not begin to explain just how much actually goes into cracking a big-league lineup. Yes, this game is largely mental. After all, it is the mental side of professional baseball that was the initial focus of this book. While it still played a large role in the examination of cup of coffee players, it became apparent that the mental side was just one aspect among a larger group of factors that affect the outcome of professional baseball players' careers.

Injuries, timing, unforeseen off-the-field circumstances, and relationships with coaches/executives all play big parts in determining how far a professional baseball player will go before they're told there is no longer room for them in the sport.

All these factors were examined within the pages of this book as you read the tales of players whose stories varied in drama and intrigue. Each player's journey shared a common thread: they were given plenty of time to think about their one day on a major-league field. Unlike longtime MLB players, most players in this book saw their careers end before they were 30. Some have come to grips with their baseball fate while others still struggle with the unknown. What if they had gotten that one extra chance?

No matter whether their big-league careers have given them a sense of closure or not, these players share another common thread: they are no longer defined by their ability to throw or hit a baseball. By design, professional ballplayers have to eat, sleep, and breathe baseball in order to reach the pinnacle of the sport. In that way, it is similar to entry-level positions in other professions.

Whether they went into real estate, business, coaching, or another field afterward, these former players' lives are no longer intertwined with their baseball playing ability. However, their playing days and unique stories of success and failure did largely shape the paths they went down after they hung up their spikes.

Now, the next generation of players gets to learn from these one-game wonders. Many of them went on to coach or still coach to this day. They get to work with players who share the dream they once had and who face the same daily struggles their mentors once did. Hopefully, through hearing these cup of coffee stories, baseball's next generation can further appreciate what it takes to get to the majors.

Perhaps more than any other sport, baseball humbles you. It's a sport centered around failure. So, in looking back on the paths of these cup of coffee players, do you think their stories are ones of success or failure? Each took a long road to get his one chance, and many faced a long road trying to get back. There are no wrong answers; the merits of their professional baseball careers are up for debate.

If you take nothing else from the interesting stories of these one-game wonders, take with you the knowledge that baseball doesn't hand you anything. Players earn what they get, and sometimes they are afforded even less than what it appears they deserve.

So, the next time you see a player making his major-league debut, take a second to appreciate the moment a little bit more. There's nothing guaranteeing that player will ever see a major-league field again. Fewer than 150 players have ended their careers with just one big-league game under their belt in the last 50 years. It is a small population, but one that will surely gain even more members in the next half century.

Hopefully, now, we have a glimpse into what those players have gone through and will continue to go through on their unique paths to the major leagues. Equipped with the firsthand stories of the players in this select group, the "invisible battle" these players face should be better appreciated by baseball fans who seek a higher understanding of what it takes to fulfill a dream shared by young boys throughout the country. It is a dream few get to see realized, and one even fewer live out for a single, fleeting day.

NOTES

INTRODUCTION

1. "Major League Historical Totals," Baseball Reference, accessed July 30, 2018.
2. "Cup of Coffee Batters," Baseball Reference, accessed July 30, 2018.
3. "Moonlight Graham," Society for Baseball Research, accessed July 30, 2018.
4. *Field of Dreams*, directed by Phil Alden Robinson (Mark Gordon Company, 1989).
5. Kevin Graham, "The First Baseball Card?," *SABR Baseball Cards* (blog), December 22, 2016.
6. "Frank Norton Stats," Baseball Reference, accessed July 30, 2018.
7. Peter Levine, "Business, Missionary Motives behind the 1888–89 World Tour," *SABR Baseball Research Journal* 13 (1984): 60–63.
8. "1871 Washington Olympics Schedule," Baseball Reference, accessed July 30, 2018.
9. "Dick Wantz," Baseball Reference, accessed July 30, 2018.
10. Bill Plunkett, "Freeway Series: Angels and Dodgers Have Built Up Some History in Their Relationship," *Orange County (CA) Register*, July 5, 2018.
11. "Cleveland Indians at California Angels Box Score, April 13, 1965," Baseball Reference, accessed July 30, 2018.
12. "Dick Wantz, Angels Hurler, Fails to Survive Operation," *Sporting News*, May 29, 1965.
13. Jon Ratliff, interview with the author.
14. Dan Barry, *Bottom of the 33rd: Hope, Redemption, and Baseball's Longest Game* (New York: Harper Perennial, 2012), 234.

15. Mike Stadler, interview with the author.

16. "Dan Osinski," Baseball Reference, accessed July 30, 2018.

17. "1967 World Series Game 7, Cardinals at Red Sox, October 12," Baseball Reference, accessed July 30, 2018.

18. "Ronny Cedeño," Baseball Reference, accessed July 30, 2018.

19. "Chase Lambin," Baseball Reference, accessed July 30, 2018.

20. "New York Mets at Houston Colt .45's Box Score, September 29, 1963," Baseball Reference, accessed July 30, 2018.

21. AP Wire, "'Dream' Start for John," *Detroit Free Press*, September 30, 1963, 1D.

22. Murray Chass, "Mets May Charge," *Ocala Star-Banner*, March 23, 1964, 11.

23. Benjamin Hoffman, "For the Sultan of Small Sample Size, a 1.000 Career Average," *New York Times*, March 30, 2013.

24. Jacqueline Howard, "The Bizarre Psychology of the Bronze Medal Win," CNN.com, August 18, 2016, accessed February 14, 2019.

25. "St. Louis Cardinals at Milwaukee Brewers Box Score, April 24, 2004," Baseball Reference, accessed July 30, 2018.

26. "Chris Saenz," Baseball Reference, accessed July 31, 2018.

27. Robert Andrews, interview with the author.

I. CHARLIE LINDSTROM

1. "Freddie Lindstrom," Baseball Reference, accessed July 30, 2018.

2. "Charlie Lindstrom," Baseball Reference, accessed July 30, 2018.

3. "American Legion Player of the Year," Baseball Almanac, accessed July 30, 2018.

4. "Ron Perranoski Trades and Transactions," Baseball Almanac, accessed July 30, 2018.

5. "1963 World Series Game 2, Dodgers at Yankees, October 3," Baseball Reference, accessed July 30, 2018.

6. "All-Time Coaches," MLB.com, accessed July 30, 2018.

7. "Bob Uecker," Baseball Reference, accessed July 30, 2018.

8. "Kansas City Athletics at Chicago White Sox Box Score, September 28, 1958," Baseball Reference, accessed July 30, 2018.

9. Stephan Benzkofer, "Go-Go White Sox of 1959 Win Pennant," *Chicago Tribune*, September 14, 2014.

10. "Lincoln College to Honor Inaugural Athletic Hall of Fame Class at Banquet," Lincoln College, November 1, 2013, accessed July 30, 2018.

2. ROE SKIDMORE

1. "Decatur, Illinois, Population 2018," World Population Review, accessed July 30, 2018.
2. "Boys Baseball Season Summaries," Illinois High School Association, accessed July 30, 2018.
3. "Roe Skidmore," Baseball Reference, accessed July 30, 2018.
4. "1968 MLB Transactions," Baseball Reference, accessed July 30, 2018.
5. "St. Louis Cardinals at Chicago Cubs Box Score, September 17, 1970," Baseball Reference, accessed July 30, 2018.
6. Bob Fallstrom, "Fallstrom: Former Eisenhower Coach Hinton Remembers Baseball Champs," *Decatur (IL) Herald and Review*, April 25, 2011.
7. "1972 Indianapolis Indians," Baseball Reference, accessed July 30, 2018.

3. LARRY YOUNT

1. "Larry Yount," Baseball Reference, accessed July 30, 2018.
2. "Atlanta Braves at Houston Astros Box Score, September 15, 1971," Baseball Reference, accessed July 30, 2018.
3. "Robin Yount," Baseball Reference, accessed July 30, 2018.
4. Paul Rubin, Dave Walker, and David Pasztor, "Buy Me Out for the Ballpark," *Phoenix New Times*, December 8, 1993.
5. Clayton Trutor, "Arizona Diamondbacks Team Ownership History," Society for American Baseball Research, last updated November 28, 2017, accessed July 30, 2018.
6. "Austin Yount," Baseball Reference, accessed July 30, 2018.
7. "Cody Yount," Baseball Reference, accessed July 30, 2018.

4. GARY MARTZ

1. Max Rieper, "Losing a Sports Team: The Relocation of the Kansas City Athletics," *SB Nation Royals Review*, January 20, 2016.
2. "Brewery Gems Profiles: Emil Sick, Brewer," Brewery Gems, accessed July 30, 2018.
3. "1969 Baseball Draft," Baseball Almanac, accessed July 30, 2018.
4. "Gary Martz," Baseball Reference, accessed July 30, 2018.
5. Matt Blitz, "The Only Major League Baseball Team to Go Bankrupt: The Story of the Seattle Pilots," *Today I Found Out* (blog), September 5, 2014.

6. "Gary Martz Trades and Transactions," Baseball Almanac, accessed July 30, 2018.

7. Bill Lamberty, "Amos Otis," Society for American Baseball Research, accessed July 30, 2018.

8. "Milwaukee Brewers at Kansas City Royals Box Score, July 8, 1975," Baseball Reference, accessed July 30, 2018.

9. "Harmon Killebrew," Baseball Reference, accessed July 30, 2018.

5. RAFAEL MONTALVO

1. "Box Score of Juan Nieves No Hitter," Baseball Almanac, accessed February 14, 2019.

2. "Rafael Montalvo Minor, Mexican, & Independent League Stats," Baseball Reference, accessed February 10, 2019.

3. "Atlanta Braves at Houston Astros Box Score, April 13, 1986," Baseball Reference, accessed February 12, 2019.

4. Bob Nightengale, "Replacement Show Goes On: Baseball: Dodgers Enter the Great Unknown Today against Yankees in Exhibition Opener," *Los Angeles Times*, March 2, 1995.

5. Mike Piazza, with Lonnie Wheeler, *Long Shot* (New York: Simon & Schuster, 2014).

6. JEFF BANISTER

1. "Jeff Banister," Baseball Reference, accessed July 30, 2018.

7. STEPHEN LARKIN

1. "Barry Larkin," Baseball Reference, accessed July 30, 2018.

2. "Byron Larkin," Sports Reference College Basketball, accessed July 30, 2018.

3. "Michael Larkin," Sports Reference College Football, accessed July 30, 2018.

4. "Stephen Larkin," Baseball Reference, accessed July 30, 2018.

5. Barry Larkin, "Games That Matter," *Players' Tribune* (blog), October 1, 2015.

6. "Pittsburgh Pirates at Cincinnati Reds Box Score, September 27, 1998," Baseball Reference, accessed July 30, 2018.

7. Larkin, "Games That Matter."

8. JON RATLIFF

1. "Chicago Cubs 1st Round Picks in the MLB June Amateur Draft," Baseball Reference, accessed July 31, 2018.

2. "Jon Ratliff," Baseball Reference, accessed July 31, 2018.

3. "Oakland Athletics at Tampa Bay Devil Rays Box Score, September 15, 2000," Baseball Reference, accessed July 31, 2018.

4. "Anaheim Angels at Oakland Athletics Box Score, September 28, 2000," Baseball Reference, accessed July 31, 2018.

9. RON WRIGHT

1. "Ron Wright," Baseball Reference, accessed July 31, 2018.

2. "Denny Neagle Trades and Transactions," Baseball Almanac, accessed July 31, 2018.

3. Steven Yeomans, "Sciatic Nerve Anatomy," Spine-Health, August 31, 2015.

4. "Seattle Mariners at Texas Rangers Box Score, April 14, 2002," Baseball Reference, accessed July 31, 2018.

5. Lee Jenkins, "The Short and Happy Career of Ron Wright," New York Times, April 15, 2007.

6. Jenkins, "The Short and Happy Career of Ron Wright."

10. SAM MARSONEK

1. "1996 MLB Draft," Baseball Almanac, accessed July 31, 2018.

2. "Sam Marsonek," Baseball Cube, accessed July 31, 2018.

3. "Sam Marsonek," Baseball Reference, accessed July 31, 2018.

4. Lawrence Rocca, "Yankees Trade Curtis to Rangers," Newsday, December 13, 1999.

5. "Tampa Bay Devil Rays at New York Yankees Box Score, July 11, 2004," Baseball Reference, accessed July 31, 2018.

6. "Eutaw, AL," Data USA, accessed July 31, 2018.

11. MATT TUPMAN

1. "Micky Ward," BoxRec, accessed July 31, 2018.

2. "2001 Division II Regionals," Baseball Reference, accessed July 31, 2018; "2002 Division II Regionals," Baseball Reference, accessed July 31, 2018.

3. "Matt Tupman," Baseball Reference, accessed July 31, 2018.

4. "Kansas City Royals Team History & Encyclopedia," Baseball Reference, accessed July 31, 2018.

5. "Kansas City Royals at Florida Marlins Box Score, May 18, 2008," Baseball Reference, accessed July 31, 2018.

6. "Kevin Gregg," Baseball Reference, accessed July 31, 2018.

7. "Kansas City Royals at Boston Red Sox Box Score, May 19, 2008," Baseball Reference, accessed July 31, 2018.

8. "California Angels at Kansas City Royals Box Score, May 15, 1973," Baseball Reference, accessed July 31, 2018.

12. OTHER "CUP OF COFFEE" STORIES

1. Gary Bedingfield, Frank Fitzpatrick, and Bill Nowlin, "Harry O'Neill," Society for American Baseball Research, accessed July 31, 2018.

2. Robert Weintraub, *The Victory Season* (New York: Back Bay Books, 2013), 27–29.

3. Weintraub, *The Victory Season.*

4. "Career Leaders & Records for Sacrifice Hits," Baseball Reference, accessed July 31, 2018.

5. Paul Mittermeyer, "Eddie Collins," Society for American Baseball Research, accessed July 31, 2018.

6. Gary Livacari, "Allan Travers," Society for American Baseball Research, accessed July 31, 2018.

7. Terry Bohn, "Bert Shepard," Society for American Baseball Research, accessed July 31, 2018.

8. Bohn, "Bert Shepard."

BIBLIOGRAPHY

Barry, Dan. *Bottom of the 33rd: Hope, Redemption, and Baseball's Longest Game*. New York: Harper Perennial, 2012.

Baseball Almanac. "1969 Baseball Draft." Accessed July 30, 2018. http://www.baseball-almanac.com/draft/baseball-draft.php?yr=1969.

———. "1996 MLB Draft." Accessed July 31, 2018. http://www.baseball-almanac.com/draft/baseball-draft.php?yr=1996.

———. "American Legion Player of the Year." Accessed July 30, 2018. http://www.baseball-almanac.com/awards/american_legion_player_of_the_year.shtml.

———. "Box Score of Juan Nieves No Hitter." Accessed February 14, 2019. http://www.baseball-almanac.com/boxscore/04151987.shtml.

———. "Denny Neagle Trades and Transactions." Accessed July 31, 2018. http://www.baseball-almanac.com/players/trades.php?p=neaglde01.

———. "Gary Martz Trades and Transactions." Accessed July 30, 2018. http://www.baseball-almanac.com/players/trades.php?p=martzga01.

———. "Ron Perranoski Trades and Transactions." Accessed July 30, 2018. http://www.baseball-almanac.com/players/trades.php?p=perraro01.

The Baseball Cube. "Sam Marsonek." Accessed July 31, 2018. http://www.thebaseballcube.com/players/profile.asp?ID=6121.

Baseball Reference. "1871 Washington Olympics Schedule." Accessed July 30, 2018. https://www.baseball-reference.com/teams/OLY/1871-schedule-scores.shtml.

———. "1963 World Series Game 2, Dodgers at Yankees, October 3." Accessed July 30, 2018. https://www.baseball-reference.com/boxes/NYA/NYA196310030.shtml.

———. "1967 World Series Game 7, Cardinals at Red Sox, October 12." Accessed July 30, 2018. https://www.baseball-reference.com/boxes/BOS/BOS196710120.shtml.

———. "1968 MLB Transactions." Accessed July 30, 2018. https://www.baseball-reference.com/leagues/MLB/1968-transactions.shtml.

———. "1972 Indianapolis Indians." Accessed July 30, 2018. https://www.baseball-reference.com/register/team.cgi?id=04cacc56.

———. "2001 Division II Regionals." Accessed July 31, 2018. https://www.baseball-reference.com/bullpen/2001_Division_II_Regionals.

———. "2002 Division II Regionals." Accessed July 31, 2018. https://www.baseball-reference.com/bullpen/2002_Division_II_Regionals.

———. "Anaheim Angels at Oakland Athletics Box Score, September 28, 2000." Accessed July 31, 2018. https://www.baseball-reference.com/boxes/OAK/OAK200009280.shtml.

———. "Atlanta Braves at Houston Astros Box Score, April 13, 1986." Accessed February 12, 2019. https://www.baseball-reference.com/boxes/HOU/HOU198604130.shtml.

———. "Atlanta Braves at Houston Astros Box Score, September 15, 1971." Accessed July 30, 2018. https://www.baseball-reference.com/boxes/HOU/HOU197109150.shtml.

———. "Austin Yount." Accessed July 30, 2018. https://www.baseball-reference.com/register/player.fcgi?id=yount-001aus.

———. "Barry Larkin." Accessed July 30, 2018. https://www.baseball-reference.com/players/l/larkiba01.shtml.

———. "Bob Uecker." Accessed July 30, 2018. https://www.baseball-reference.com/players/u/ueckebo01.shtml.

———. "California Angels at Kansas City Royals Box Score, May 15, 1973." Accessed July 31, 2018. https://www.baseball-reference.com/boxes/KCA/KCA197305150.shtml.

———. "Career Leaders & Records for Sacrifice Hits." Accessed July 31, 2018. https://www.baseball-reference.com/leaders/SH_career.shtml.

———. "Charlie Lindstrom." Accessed July 30, 2018. https://www.baseball-reference.com/players/l/lindsch02.shtml.

———. "Chase Lambin." Accessed July 30, 2018. https://www.baseball-reference.com/register/player.fcgi?id=lambin001cha.

———. "Chicago Cubs 1st Round Picks in the MLB June Amateur Draft." Accessed July 31, 2018. https://www.baseball-reference.com/draft/index.fcgi?team_ID=CHC&draft_round=1s&draft_type=junreg&query_type=franch_round.

———. "Chris Saenz." Accessed July 31, 2018. https://www.baseball-reference.com/players/s/saenzch01.shtml.

———."Cleveland Indians at California Angels Box Score, April 13, 1965." Accessed July 30, 2018. https://www.baseball-reference.com/boxes/CAL/CAL196504130.shtml.

———. "Cody Yount." Accessed July 30, 2018. https://www.baseball-reference.com/register/player.fcgi?id=yount-000cod.

———. "Cup of Coffee Batters." Accessed July 30, 2018. https://www.baseball-reference.com/friv/batters-coffee.shtml.

———. "Dan Osinski." Accessed July 30, 2018. https://www.baseball-reference.com/players/o/osinsda01.shtml.

———. "Dick Wantz." Accessed July 30, 2018. https://www.baseball-reference.com/players/w/wantzdi01.shtml.

———. "Frank Norton Stats." Accessed July 30, 2018. https://www.baseball-reference.com/players/n/nortofr01.shtml.

———. "Freddie Lindstrom." Accessed July 30, 2018. https://www.baseball-reference.com/players/l/lindsfr01.shtml.

———. "Gary Martz." Accessed July 30, 2018. https://www.baseball-reference.com/players/m/martzga01.shtml.

———. "Harmon Killebrew." Accessed July 30, 2018. https://www.baseball-reference.com/players/k/killeha01.shtml.

———. "Jeff Banister." Accessed July 30, 2018. https://www.baseball-reference.com/players/b/banisje01.shtml.

———. "Jon Ratliff." Accessed July 31, 2018. https://www.baseball-reference.com/players/r/ratlijo01.shtml.

———. "Kansas City Athletics at Chicago White Sox Box Score, September 28, 1958." Accessed July 30, 2018. https://www.baseball-reference.com/boxes/CHA/CHA195809280.shtml.

———. "Kansas City Royals at Boston Red Sox Box Score, May 19, 2008." Accessed July 31, 2018. https://www.baseball-reference.com/boxes/BOS/BOS200805190.shtml.

———. "Kansas City Royals at Florida Marlins Box Score, May 18, 2008." Accessed July 31, 2018. https://www.baseball-reference.com/boxes/FLO/FLO200805180.shtml.

———. "Kansas City Royals Team History & Encyclopedia." Accessed July 31, 2018. https://www.baseball-reference.com/teams/KCR/.

———. "Kevin Gregg." Accessed July 31, 2018. https://www.baseball-reference.com/players/g/greggke01.shtml.

———. "Larry Yount." Accessed July 30, 2018. https://www.baseball-reference.com/players/y/yountla01.shtml.

―――. "Major League Historical Totals." Accessed July 30, 2018. https://www.baseball-reference.com/leagues/index.shtml.

―――. "Matt Tupman." Accessed July 31, 2018. https://www.baseball-reference.com/players/t/tupmama01.shtml.

―――. "Milwaukee Brewers at Kansas City Royals Box Score, July 8, 1975." Accessed July 30, 2018. https://www.baseball-reference.com/boxes/KCA/KCA197507080.shtml.

―――. "New York Mets at Houston Colt .45's Box Score, September 29, 1963." Accessed July 30, 2018. https://www.baseball-reference.com/boxes/HOU/HOU196309290.shtml.

―――. "Oakland Athletics at Tampa Bay Devil Rays Box Score, September 15, 2000." Accessed July 31, 2018. https://www.baseball-reference.com/boxes/TBA/TBA200009150.shtml.

―――. "Pittsburgh Pirates at Cincinnati Reds Box Score, September 27, 1998." Accessed July 30, 2018. https://www.baseball-reference.com/boxes/CIN/CIN199809270.shtml.

―――. "Rafael Montalvo Minor, Mexican, & Independent League Stats." Accessed February 10, 2019. https://www.baseball-reference.com/players/m/montara01.shtml.

―――. "Robin Yount." Accessed July 30, 2018. https://www.baseball-reference.com/players/y/yountro01.shtml.

―――. "Roe Skidmore." Accessed July 30, 2018. https://www.baseball-reference.com/players/s/skidmro01.shtml.

―――. "Ron Wright." Accessed July 31, 2018. https://www.baseball-reference.com/players/w/wrighro02.shtml.

―――. "Ronny Cedeño." Accessed July 30, 2018. https://www.baseball-reference.com/players/c/cedenro02.shtml.

―――. "Sam Marsonek." Accessed July 31, 2018. https://www.baseball-reference.com/players/m/marsosa01.shtml.

―――. "Seattle Mariners at Texas Rangers Box Score, April 14, 2002." Accessed July 31, 2018. https://www.baseball-reference.com/boxes/TEX/TEX200204140.shtml.

―――. "St. Louis Cardinals at Chicago Cubs Box Score, September 17, 1970." Accessed July 30, 2018. https://www.baseball-reference.com/boxes/CHN/CHN197009170.shtml.

―――. "St. Louis Cardinals at Milwaukee Brewers Box Score, April 24, 2004." Accessed July 30, 2018. https://www.baseball-reference.com/boxes/MIL/MIL200404240.shtml.

―――. "Stephen Larkin." Accessed July 30, 2018. https://www.baseball-reference.com/players/l/larkist02.shtml.

―――. "Tampa Bay Devil Rays at New York Yankees Box Score, July 11, 2004." Accessed July 31, 2018. https://www.baseball-reference.com/boxes/NYA/NYA200407110.shtml.

Bedingfield, Gary, Frank Fitzpatrick, and Bill Nowlin. "Harry O'Neill." Society for American Baseball Research. Accessed July 31, 2018. https://sabr.org/bioproj/person/44e9cdff.

Benzkofer, Stephan. "Go-Go White Sox of 1959 Win Pennant." *Chicago Tribune*, September 14, 2014.

Blitz, Matt. "The Only Major League Baseball Team to Go Bankrupt: The Story of the Seattle Pilots." *Today I Found Out* (blog). September 5, 2014.

Bohn, Terry. "Bert Shepard." Society for American Baseball Research. Accessed July 31, 2018. https://sabr.org/bioproj/person/8cb03c17.

BoxRec. "Micky Ward." Accessed July 31, 2018. http://boxrec.com/en/boxer/3603.

Brewery Gems. "Brewery Gems Profiles: Emil Sick, Brewer." Accessed July 30, 2018. http://www.brewerygems.com/emil.htm.

Data USA. "Eutaw, AL." Accessed July 31, 2018. https://datausa.io/profile/geo/eutaw-al/.

"Dick Wantz, Angels Hurler, Fails to Survive Operation." *Sporting News*, May 29, 1965.

Fallstrom, Bob. "Fallstrom: Former Eisenhower Coach Hinton Remembers Baseball Champs." *Decatur (IL) Herald and Review*, April 25, 2011.

Filippino, Marc. "The Road Warriors Take the Idea of a Traveling Sports Team to the Extreme." NPR, *All Things Considered.* May 29, 2018. Accessed February 14, 2019. https://www.npr.org/2018/05/29/615263445/the-road-warriors-take-the-idea-of-a-travelling-sports-team-to-the-extreme.

Graham, Kevin. "The First Baseball Card?" *SABR Baseball Cards* (blog). December 22, 2016. https://sabrbaseballcards.blog/2016/12/22/the-first-baseball-card/.

Hoffman, Benjamin. "For the Sultan of Small Sample Size, a 1.000 Career Average." *New York Times*, March 30, 2013.

Howard, Jacqueline. "The Bizarre Psychology of the Bronze Medal Win." CNN.com. August 18, 2016. Accessed February 14, 2019. https://www.cnn.com/2016/08/18/health/bronze-medal-psychology-olympics/index.html.

Illinois High School Association. "Boys Baseball Season Summaries." Accessed July 30, 2018. https://www.ihsa.org/SportsActivities/BoysBaseball/RecordsHistory.aspx?url=/data/ba/records/index.htm.

Lamberty, Bill. "Amos Otis." Society for American Baseball Research. Accessed July 30, 2018. https://sabr.org/bioproj/person/588ccedb.

Larkin, Barry. "Games That Matter." *Players' Tribune* (blog). October 1, 2015. https://www.theplayerstribune.com/en-us/articles/barry-larkin-brother-stephen-reds-1998.

Levine, Peter. "Business, Missionary Motives behind the 1888–89 World Tour." *SABR Baseball Research Journal* 13 (1984): 60–63.

Lincoln College. "Lincoln College to Honor Inaugural Athletic Hall of Fame Class at Banquet." November 1, 2013. Accessed July 30, 2018. https://lincolncollege.edu/lincoln-college-honor-inaugural-athletic-hall-fame-class-banquet/.

Livacari, Gary. "Allan Travers." Society for American Baseball Research. Accessed July 31, 2018. https://sabr.org/bioproj/person/8b444434.

Mittermeyer, Paul. "Eddie Collins." Society for American Baseball Research. Accessed July 31, 2018. https://sabr.org/bioproj/person/c480756d.

MLB.com. "All-Time Coaches." Accessed July 30, 2018. https://www.mlb.com/dodgers/history/all-time-coaches.

Nightengale, Bob. "Replacement Show Goes On: Baseball: Dodgers Enter the Great Unknown Today against Yankees in Exhibition Opener." *Los Angeles Times*, March 2, 1995.

Piazza, Mike. *Long Shot.* With Lonnie Wheeler. New York: Simon & Schuster, 2014.

Plunkett, Bill. "Freeway Series: Angels and Dodgers Have Built Up Some History in Their Relationship." *Orange County (CA) Register*, July 5, 2018.

Rieper, Max. "Losing a Sports Team: The Relocation of the Kansas City Athletics." *SB Nation Royals Review*, January 20, 2016.

Robinson, Phil Alden, dir. *Field of Dreams.* Mark Gordon Company, 1989.

Rocca, Lawrence. "Yankees Trade Curtis to Rangers." *Newsday*, December 13, 1999.

Rubin, Paul, Dave Walker, and David Pasztor. "Buy Me Out for the Ballpark." *Phoenix New Times*, December 8, 1993.

Society for American Baseball Research. "Moonlight Graham." Accessed July 30, 2018. https://sabr.org/bioproj/person/a054b3d6.

Sports Reference College Basketball. "Byron Larkin." Accessed July 30, 2018. https://www.sports-reference.com/cbb/players/byron-larkin-1.html.

Sports Reference College Football. "Michael Larkin." Accessed July 30, 2018. https://www.sports-reference.com/cfb/players/mike-larkin-1.html.

Trutor, Clayton. "Arizona Diamondbacks Team Ownership History." Society for American Baseball Research. Last updated November 28, 2017. Accessed July 30, 2018. https://sabr.org/research/arizona-diamondbacks-team-ownership-history.

Weintraub, Robert. *The Victory Season.* New York: Back Bay Books, 2013.

World Population Review. "Decatur, Illinois Population 2018." Accessed July 30, 2018. http://worldpopulationreview.com/us-cities/decatur-il-population/.

Yeomans, Steven. "Sciatic Nerve Anatomy." Spine-Health. August 31, 2015. https://www.spine-health.com/conditions/spine-anatomy/sciatic-nerve-anatomy.

INDEX

ABOUT THE AUTHOR

Jacob Kornhauser is a die-hard Chicago Cubs fan who grew up 30 miles from Wrigley Field. His passion for baseball led him into sportswriting for such publications as Bleacher Report and FanSided, a subsidiary of *Sports Illustrated*. He has covered sports for local television stations in Missouri and Oregon, and his career has led him to work for two of the largest sports media companies in the country: ESPN and FOX Sports. He lives in Los Angeles, California, with his girlfriend, Khaki, and hopes that unlike the fleeting MLB careers of the unique men chronicled in *The Cup of Coffee Club*, this book—his first—is not also his last.